# War and Drought in Sudan

# War and Drought in Sudan

## Essays on Population Displacement

Edited by Eltigani E. Eltigani

Foreword by Carolyn Fluehr-Lobban

**University Press of Florida**
*Gainesville/Tallahassee/Tampa/Boca Raton*
*Pensacola/Orlando/Miami/Jacksonville*

Printed in the United States of America on acid-free paper ∞


00 99 98 97 96 95  6 5 4 3 2 1

Library of Congress Cataloging-in-Publication Data

War and drought in Sudan: essays on population displacement/edited
by Eltigani E. Eltigani.
p. cm.
Includes bibliographical references (p. ) and index.
ISBN 0-8130-1336-4 (alk. paper)
1. Migration, Internal—Sudan. 2. Sudan—History, Military.
3. Droughts—Sudan. 4. Famines—Sudan. 5. Refugees—Sudan.
6. Sudan—Economic conditions. 7. Sudan—Social conditions.
I. Eltigani, Eltigani El Tahir.
HB2121.8.A3W37 1995
304.8′09624—dc20 94-34182

The University Press of Florida is the scholarly publishing agency for the State University System of Florida, comprised of Florida A & M University, Florida Atlantic University, Florida International University, Florida State University, University of Central Florida, University of Florida, University of North Florida, University of South Florida, and University of West Florida.

University Press of Florida
15 Northwest 15th Street
Gainesville, FL 32611

# Contents

# Figures

# Tables

# Foreword

*Carolyn Fluehr-Lobban*

Because of drought, political instability, civil wars, and resulting famines, all of which have plagued northeast Africa and the Horn, the attention of the world has been focused for the past decade on the African cases of Ethiopia, Somalia, and Sudan. In Europe and southwest Asia, the plight of the Bosnians, the Palestinians, the Kurds, and the Afghanis has heightened awareness in the West regarding the practical and political problems of refugees. The case of Sudan, however, is probably one of the least well known, primarily because successive governments have denied the occurrence of famine and displacement of people, and journalists' freedom to report on events in Sudan has been circumscribed. Even though the drought that afflicted Ethiopia in the early 1980s also deeply affected Sudan, Western media attention was directed at Ethiopia. Likewise, Somalia's more recent case of civil war and man-made famine has resulted in U.S. and Western intervention, unprecedented in postcolonial times, while Sudan with its own civil war and widespread famine remains, for the most part, out of the headlines.

This book on population displacement in Sudan during the past decade is both timely and of wide relevance to the region and global events. As a volume comprised entirely of Sudanese contributors, it is unique. The majority of the authors are from Gezira University, which has specialized in rural sociology and development questions; and the writers themselves have witnessed the effects of Sudanese displacement.

The immediate background of the current crisis in Sudan is the ascendancy of a politicized Islam since 1983. Previously, Sudan had been famous in Africa for its reception of political refugees, not for the creation of its own generation of refugees. The wars and political turmoil in Uganda, Eritrea, and Ethiopia at large and the disturbances in Chad, Zaire, and the Central African Republic brought large numbers of refugees into the country, fleeing to the relative safety and security of Sudan across its enormous borders. During the decade of peace between the major Sudanese civil wars (approximately 1972–82), Sudan played host to an estimated one million refugees, a figure said to be the largest in any African nation at the time and making Khartoum a major post for the United Nations Commission for Refugees. For the most part, these refugees were accepted by the Sudanese government without prejudice, except for the periodic removal of refugees, especially Eritreans, from urban areas to more remote refugee camps. Once civil war between the north and south resumed, the acceptance of Eritrean refugees was politically balanced by the renewed flow of southern Sudanese refugees into Ethiopia; and the two governments had an understanding that each refugee population was to be tolerated.

This Sudanese reputation for hospitality to refugee populations was called into serious question when it was compared with the treatment of the country's own internal refugee populations, who were primarily victims of the renewal of civil war in the southern part of the country and the aftermath of generalized violence and terror in what had once been relatively peaceful areas. These events all occurred after the breakdown of the Addis Ababa Accords between the central government and the southern Sudanese, which in themselves had ended a period of civil war between 1955 and 1972. The second round of civil war was signaled by President Nimeiri's unilateral abrogation of the terms of the agreement, his declaration that Islamic law was to become state law, and the creation of a new movement, Sudan's People's Liberation Movement/Army (SPLM/SPLA), which called for a national democracy based on secularism and regional representation. Trust and confidence between the central government and the southerners had been eroding for some time before 1983, especially after oil was discovered in the south. President Nimeiri decided to refine the oil in the north and export it for hard currency, thus leaving little in the way of promised economic development for the south.

The renewed outbreak of war set into motion new forces in the southwestern part of the country, where government-armed militias were reported to have seized control of territories north of the Bahr al-Ghazal region, an area into which many southerners had fled from the war in the south. This action also led to intense tribal warfare in the regions of Kordofan and Darfur.

Refugees poured into Khartoum from the affected areas, including the southern and western parts of the country. Sudanese refugees were probably treated worse than foreign refugee populations because they were granted no official recognition or status by the central government. The government under Nimeiri denied the existence of the natural drought and famine affecting western and eastern Sudan during the early 1980s, and the subsequent governments of Sadiq El Mahadi and General Al Bashir have denied the current man-made famine and dislocation of people caused by civil war. Relief efforts have not been government-initiated but have come into the country as a result of international pressure regarding the plight of Sudan's own refugees. The UN relief effort, Operation Life-line Sudan, was repeatedly granted and then denied permission to work in the south. Other Western relief agencies have been accused of proselytizing and using relief as a tool of conversion, thus making humanitarian relief efforts highly politicized.

The renewed violence and resulting population displacement have not appeared to soften any of the four separate governments that have ruled since 1983 (including the one-year transitional government that held power between the Nimeiri and El Mahadi regimes); and each has failed to negotiate an end to the war and an adequate political solution to the issue of equality and democratic representation of southerners in a unified Sudan. Each government has pursued the idea that military victory is possible and that the war will remain confined to the south. Serious negotiations between the central governments in Khartoum and the SPLM/SPLA have failed to materialize, despite the fact that each of the regimes represents quite different political orientations. The recent split in the southern movement has provided yet another rationale for the failure of a round of peace talks in Abuja, which was hosted by the Nigerian government during 1991–92: the Khartoum government has claimed that it does not know with which southern movement it is negotiating.

In lieu of a political solution, the spread of violence has continued and the number of internal refugees has steadily increased throughout the 1980s into the 1990s. The world knows little of the current devastation in Sudan because of the official denial of a famine or refugee problem, the resulting restriction of media access to the affected areas, and the curtailment of the relief efforts of various international agencies. This book effectively documents the devastation that Sudan has experienced as a result of chronic civil war and natural disaster. The economic drain on the country as a result of the war represents a tremendous loss of precious potential development capital. And the loss in human terms is almost incalculable: the casualties of war; the children without families and without hope of education; the displacement of rural farmers and pastoralists and the disruption or destruction of their economy; the reduction in productivity of a country drained by war; the devolution of virtually every human service, from education and health to the availability of food and commodities; and the loss of Sudan's most precious resource—its people (from the most educated to the simplest farmer or herder)—who have been forced to flee the country by the hundreds of thousands as a result of economic hardship or political disturbance.

The lessons learned from the tragic case of Sudan can be useful to the region and to the world as a whole.

# Introduction

*Eltigani E. Eltigani*

Sudan is the largest country in Africa, with a total area of one million square miles and a population estimated at 24.9 million in 1993. The country is endowed with rich natural resources that include abundant arable land, water, mineral resources, and oil.

Nevertheless, despite Sudan's enormous potential, the Sudanese people have been plagued by poverty and, since the early 1980s, by persistent famine. The Sudanese economy has deteriorated steadily since the late 1970s, manifested by the fact that per capita income has declined from $430 in 1980 to $300 in 1990. The country's foreign debt has soared from $308 million in 1970 to an estimated $12 billion (including principal, interest, and arrears) in the late 1980s. The ratio of outstanding debt to the gross national product (GNP) increased from 19.6 percent in 1973 to 130.4 percent in 1984 and to 162.6 percent by the end of 1987. Inflation showed a greater increase in 1988–89 than ever before. In December 1988 the International Monetary Fund (IMF) estimated a rate of inflation of 80 percent, twice the average rate of 1987–88. Inflation reached 100 percent by the end of 1989 and has increased steadily ever since.

The deterioration in the economic conditions of the country has been exacerbated by the severe drought conditions during most of the 1980s and early 1990s. The regions hardest hit by the drought and desertification fall mainly between 12 and 18 degrees north, an area of 650,000 square kilometers that constitutes 25 percent of the total area of Sudan. The region affected by the drought produces 90 percent of the country's agricultural crops, 95 percent of food crops and oil seeds, and 85 percent of firewood.

Millions of small-scale and subsistence farmers and animal herders have been affected. During 1984–85 it was estimated that at least 2.4 million people lived in areas affected by the famine. It was also reported that several thousand people perished due to famine by mid-1985 and that 1.3 million persons (most of them children) experienced severe malnutrition. Most of the people affected by the drought and famine were forced to leave their home areas and migrate to other parts of the country looking for food.

Coinciding with the drought was the outbreak of civil war in the south in mid-1983, which destroyed the resource base of the rural southern population. Entire communities were rendered homeless. Some of the displaced southern population sought refuge in the north; others crossed the border into neighboring countries (Ethiopia, Zaire, Uganda, and Kenya).

The enormity of the population displacement crisis is borne out by the fact that almost a third of Sudan's population is currently displaced. This massive population displacement is primarily an outcome of the interaction of underdevelopment, misguided development policies, environmental degradation, and armed conflict. It has been argued that the interaction of these factors makes Sudan similar to a weakened body whose lowered resistance to disease renders it more susceptible to illness.[1]

The crisis of population displacement has exposed the weaknesses of the Sudanese political and economic structures. Since the country gained political independence in 1956, the Sudanese political scene has been marked by instability and a succession of multiparty sectarian governments and military regimes. The successive political leaderships of the country have failed to produce a formula in which all segments of Sudanese society are represented politically and are guaranteed a share in national wealth. As a result, not only have the issues of political representation, regional disparities in socioeconomic development, and share of national wealth never been seriously addressed, but more complex issues have been introduced to add to the instability of the system.

Issues of contention include the national identity of the country and the role of religion in the state. It is tragic that after more than thirty years of political independence Sudan is still searching for its identity and a form of political structure that ensures stability and economic well-being for its citizens. The failure to address and find peaceful and political solutions to these issues has created built-in political instability and armed conflict between the central governments in Khartoum and the rebel movements in southern Sudan. The armed conflict led to the loss of thousands of lives of both southern and northern Sudanese, strained national unity, drained the country's natural and financial resources (which could have been spent on the economic and social development of the country), and led to the displacement of a sizable portion of the southern Sudanese population.

The weakness of the country's economic structure stems from the design of its development strategy. Since independence, the successive socioeconomic plans (starting with the Ten-year Plan, 1960–61 to 1970–71) were geared toward the development of large-scale agricultural projects. Investments, by both private and public sectors, were directed toward the development and expansion of the modern sector (both agricultural and industrial) and the complete neglect of the traditional sector that engages 70 percent of Sudan's population. The expansion of the modern agricultural sector was not based on modernizing the traditional sector through changes in land tenure laws, provision of credit, and other essential technical inputs to improve productivity and the standard of living of the rural population. Instead, the development polices were aimed at the elimination of the traditional sector altogether. The irrationality of this approach was pointed out by an International Labor Organization mission to Sudan. It argued that in equity terms, traditional agriculture and livestock raising are clearly the most promising modes of development, both with regard to increasing incomes in these activities and improving standards of living among the nation's poorest people. The development of traditional agriculture and livestock in the west and south—especially if accompanied by the expansion of public services such as education, health, and water supplies—would contribute significantly to containing and even reducing interregional differences. On the other hand, the development of mechanized, rain-fed agriculture creates a small number of very high income earners, while irrigation creates middle-income tenants.[2]

The expansion of large-scale commercial agriculture projects (both irrigated and rain-fed) devoted to the production of cash crops for export was undertaken without regard for ecological consequences.

As a result, the population of the traditional rural sector was driven to marginal areas with a poor resource base; hence, their livelihood became vulnerable to changes in environmental conditions. Some of the displaced rural population became agricultural laborers, while others moved to the urban centers to join the ever-growing informal sector.

The ultimate result of the development strategies pursued by the successive governments has been the consolidation of sharp regional disparities in levels of development, the sharpening of the socioeconomic dualism that these policies were purportedly attempting to alleviate, and the creation of a built-in potential of displacement for the rural population. The crisis of population displacement came to a head after the 1984 drought that devastated the regions of Darfur and Kordofan (western Sudan) and the eastern region, although signs of the impending crisis had been visible since the poor rainy seasons of 1982 and 1983. As a result of the drought and the failure of subsistence crops produced by the traditional sector, prices of staple food crops such as sorghum and millet skyrocketed, while the prices of livestock dropped sharply as more nomads started to sell their animals. This significantly reduced the ability of a sizable segment of the traditional rural population to buy food and hence exposed them to starvation.

Since 1984, the attitude of the successive governments toward the displaced population has been marked by denial, indifference, and outright hostility. The displaced have been viewed as a threat to political stability, a source of social and cultural tension, and a burden on the deteriorating urban economy. Those who move to the national capital and other urban centers have been denied access to adequate shelter and social services in an effort to discourage them from permanently settling there. Furthermore, a policy of forcibly relocating the displaced to their regions of origin or to outlying parts of the national capital has been consistently pursued ever since the mid-1980s.

President Nimeiri was very reluctant, despite the urging of many international organizations, to declare a state of emergency and request food aid to avert the 1984 famine. His reluctance was mainly dictated by political considerations: he found it embarrassing to acknowledge the existence of famine in a country he was trying to project as the potential breadbasket of Africa and Arabia. A state of emergency was declared only after he could no longer resist international and internal pressures.

By 1984, towns in the south and southwest had already begun receiving large influxes of people escaping the military conflict in the south. Nimeiri's security forces attempted to prevent the drought victims of Kordofan and Darfur from reaching the western periphery of the capital, Khartoum. Nevertheless, some managed to reach and reside in the unplanned parts of western Omdurman such as El Muwelih.

In his attempt to break the internal isolation and growing discontent with his regime, Nimeiri tried to find a scapegoat to blame for the deteriorating conditions in the urban centers, particularly in Khartoum. Choosing the displaced population in Khartoum, he instituted the policy of *el Kesha* (forced relocation): the displaced who trekked to Khartoum from western and southern Sudan were randomly picked up by security forces and relocated either back to their places of origin or to production sites in the districts of the central region.

The transitional military government, established after the Nimeiri regime was toppled in April 1985, set up the Squatter Settlements Abolition Organ; and guidelines were issued regarding the categorization of all occupants of government land in Khartoum. The first category was the *squatters*—those who had come to Khartoum before 1984. The second category was the *displaced*, which included all those who had moved to Khartoum because of the drought in the west or the war in the south. Household surveys were conducted in the squatter settlements to determine duration of stay in Khartoum and type of employment. Duration of residence and employment were considered the major determining factors in eligibility for alternative plots of land in Khartoum. Under this policy the displaced were not eligible for alternative plots because they were considered temporary residents.

The eligibility criteria for land allocation have been fraught with methodological and practical problems. For example, using a cutoff date to categorize people into displaced and economic migrants is wrong in principle. Rural-urban migration is still continuing, and any assumption that it stopped in 1984 or that those migrants who arrived after 1984 are exclusively famine or war-affected is erroneous. Furthermore, the decision to distinguish in terms of land entitlement between economic migrants and crisis-induced migrants can easily be regarded as discrimination, which becomes more evident when one learns that the displaced are the more economically underprivileged of the two groups.

In 1988, the coalition government of Sadiq El Mahdi established the Commission of the Displaced (COD). Toward the end of that year, the COD started experimenting with resettlement projects to relocate the displaced from urban areas to the agriculturally productive areas of Renk and Wad Dakona (White Nile Province). These projects, however, left much to be desired in terms of proper formulation, design, implementation, and management.

By the end of 1988, interest in dealing with the crisis of displacement led to collaboration between the COD, the United Nations Development Program (UNDP), the United States Agency for International Development (USAID), and several nongovernmental organizations (NGOs) operating through the Displaced Task Force. In addition to providing policy advice and technical assistance (mainly information from UNDP to COD and the Ministry of Social Welfare), the group also dealt with the tedious task of monitoring the situation of the displaced who had escaped from military activities in the south to the White Nile, Blue Nile, South Kordofan, and South Darfur provinces. By the beginning of 1989, the government of Sudan was encouraged to adopt a policy toward displacement based on (1) the recognition of the need to integrate some of the displaced into the urban socioeconomic fabric, (2) the need to rehabilitate secure homelands properly in preparation for the resettlement of those willing to return, and (3) the right of the displaced in urban areas to access adequate food, water, health, education, and other municipal services without being harassed.

By March 1989, the international community decided to concentrate all efforts on the plight of civilians still caught in the conflict in the south. As a result, Operation Life-line Sudan (OLS) successfully shifted international attention to those civilians. At the same time, however, political and administrative squabbling meant that policy advice and promises of technical assistance from the United Nations and other international bodies were neglected. Government institutions, once engaged in a promising dialogue, abandoned it and began implementing their own ideas of assistance to the displaced; and the inevitable political friction inherent in OLS made the government less receptive to advice even on otherwise noncontroversial issues.

The military government that took power in June 1989 convened the National Conference on Displacement in March 1990. The policy recommendations submitted by the conference were based on three premises: (1) returning the displaced to agriculturally productive areas near their original homes (which essentially meant moving them to transitional areas or to government schemes such as the Kenana sugar project), (2) moving the displaced to home areas declared safe by the government, and (3) relocating the displaced from Khartoum to the city's periphery. Following these recommendations, the COD started the policy of forced relocation of the displaced. This policy was criticized on the grounds that it did not solicit the cooperation of the displaced population and did not involve it in the timing and selection of relocation sites; in addition, the relocation sites were not properly equipped with shelters and other essential services. Thus, it was natural that the displaced people resisted forced relocation attempts. Most returned to their old settlements because of their inability to make a living in the new sites, and the few who remained in these sites depended heavily on relief provided by NGOs to survive.

The massive population displacement in Sudan and the way it has been handled by the Sudan government and the multilateral agencies provide an illuminating lesson that we can use when addressing population displacement problems in other countries experiencing political and social turmoil. This volume is a collection of essays that attempts to shed some light on the crisis of population displacement in Sudan in hopes of contributing to a systematic understanding of the various dimensions and ramifications of the current crisis. The arguments presented by the contributors point to the fact that the current displacement crisis in Sudan is rooted in the misguided development strategies pursued by the successive governments of the country, which in turn have led to the marginalization of large segments of the Sudanese society. The essays also argue that the regimes' policies toward the displaced, which include the institutions created to deal with this population, have actually intensified rather than alleviated the plight of the displaced people.

Abu Sin's essay (chapter 1) deals with the environmental causes and implications of population displacement in Sudan. He considers the country's ecosystem as an essential contributing factor of the population displacement process. In addition, he argues that Sudan's colonial heritage and its postindependence economic policies are also important factors contributing to population displacement in Sudan.

In chapter 2, Hassaballa and Eltigani's essay continues Abu Sin's discussion by analyzing two case studies (the Gezira Scheme and the Kenana Sugar Company). The authors argue that the colonial mode of production, which aimed primarily at exploiting local resources, transformed the traditional subsistence economy into an export-oriented one. The establishment of large-scale commercial agriculture to produce export crops created the potential for population displacement and the migration of rural people. These trends were reinforced during the postindependence era when national governments adopted identical development strategies.

El Shazali discusses the sociocultural dimensions of displacement in chapter 3. He argues that the rapid social change experienced by the displaced population is a process of alienation, extraction, and abstraction from cultural roots that provide symbolic meaning for existence as well as mechanisms of social control and interaction. Such processes undoubtedly have social-revolutionary potential; but in the absence of conducive socioeconomic conditions, the consequences may be antirevolutionary and counterproductive.

Wol's essay (chapter 4) examines the absorption of displaced students from southern Sudan into northern schools, particularly those in Khartoum. He outlines some of the obstacles facing the effort to provide schooling for those displaced southern students.

In chapter 5, Eltigani discusses the health problems facing the displaced population in settlements in greater Khartoum and the underlying factors that may contribute to observed health conditions. He also discusses the health delivery systems in selected displaced settlements around Khartoum.

Mahran examines the issues of displacement, food aid, and national security in chapter 6. He establishes that the drought of 1984–85 had a significant negative impact on food production; as a result, the degree of dependency on food aid has increased. He argues that despite its humanitarian intent, food aid has shaken up long-established traditions in Sudanese society. Attitudes of dependency have developed, not only among ordinary citizens but at the level of the national government, and the government has used food aid to solve short-term problems, thereby diverting the attention of policymakers away from long-term agricultural development.

In chapter 7, Elmugly provides a critical assessment of the institutional structures created by the Sudanese governments to handle the problem of the displaced population. His analysis sheds some light on the viability and fitness of these institutions for handling the crisis situation caused by the displacement of millions of people.

Eltom's essay (chapter 8) examines how the UNDP, the UN Emergency Unit, and other UN agencies currently view the issue of displacement and its various ramifications in Sudan. He outlines agency attempts to alleviate the plight of the displaced population in Sudan and shows how the enormity of the displacement problem has challenged the entire United Nations system, eventually forcing it to modify much of its mandate and development strategies.

In chapter 9, Eltigani recommends ways to address the crisis of population displacement in Sudan.

Chapter 1

# Environmental Causes and Implications of Population Displacement in Sudan

*M. E. Abu Sin*

Population displacement is a process through which a mass of people change their place of residence due to sudden causes or an accumulation of causes. Many terms have been used to describe this phenomenon, including population uprooting, depopulation, mass population mobility, and population exodus. Displacement is a strong indicator of the lack of a sustainable environmental resource base, production system, cultural setting, and political setting. Although it is a form of migration, it remains distinct because of its excessive volume and because it involves people who have a low propensity to migrate.

Displacement as a form of migration is a way to adjust to environmental stress, whether sudden or gradual—an interaction between the individual, the community, and the environment. As a form of sudden mass mobility, it has become a common and disturbing factor in contemporary Africa, particularly in the parts of the continent subject to desertification, regional wars, and disputes.

In Africa, it is not easy to identify simple reasons for displacement, either within a nation or between states. Most, however, are related to natural resources or to political instability (figs. 1.1 and 1.2).

Part of the savanna belt, Sudan has excellent potential for population support, yet it is one of Africa's most affected countries in terms of population displacement. This is due, in part, to environmental reasons, lack of proper planning, and political instability (such as the southern Sudan war).

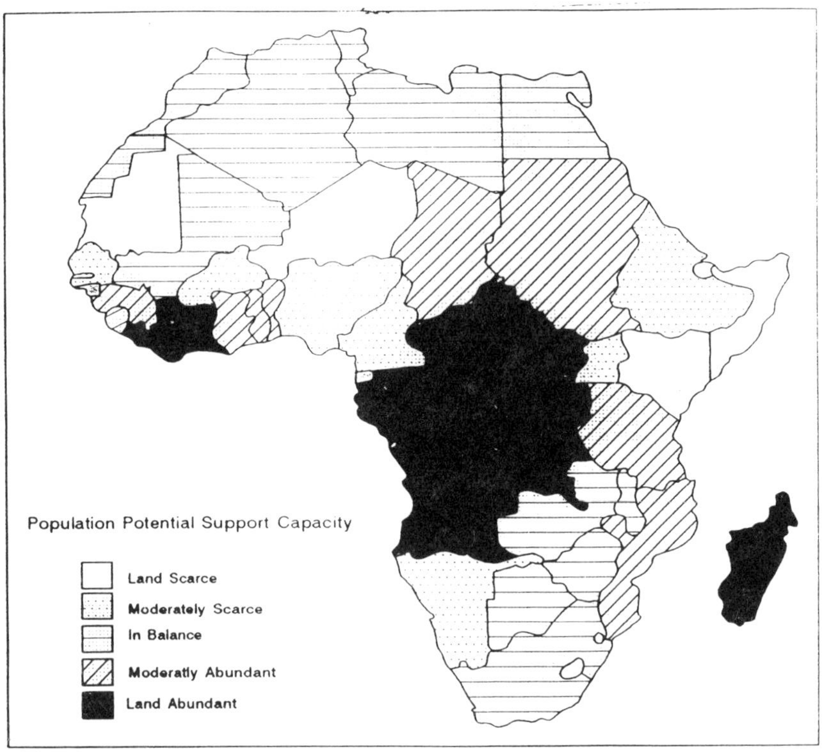


Figure 1.1. Potential population support capacity in Africa. Source: M.E. Abu Sin (1990).

Keeping these considerations in mind, I will review the following issues related to Sudan's population displacement crisis:

- Sudan's environment as a factor of displacement
- The causes of displacement, both natural and man-made
- Environmental implications and suggested policy guidelines relevant to the issue

This chapter is primarily concerned with Sudanese nationals as displaced people; I do not consider refugees from neighboring countries despite their important influence on population fluidity and distribution. During the past decade, the displacement of nationals has become increasingly important in population trends and patterns and has affected concentration, integration, the economy, and quality of life.

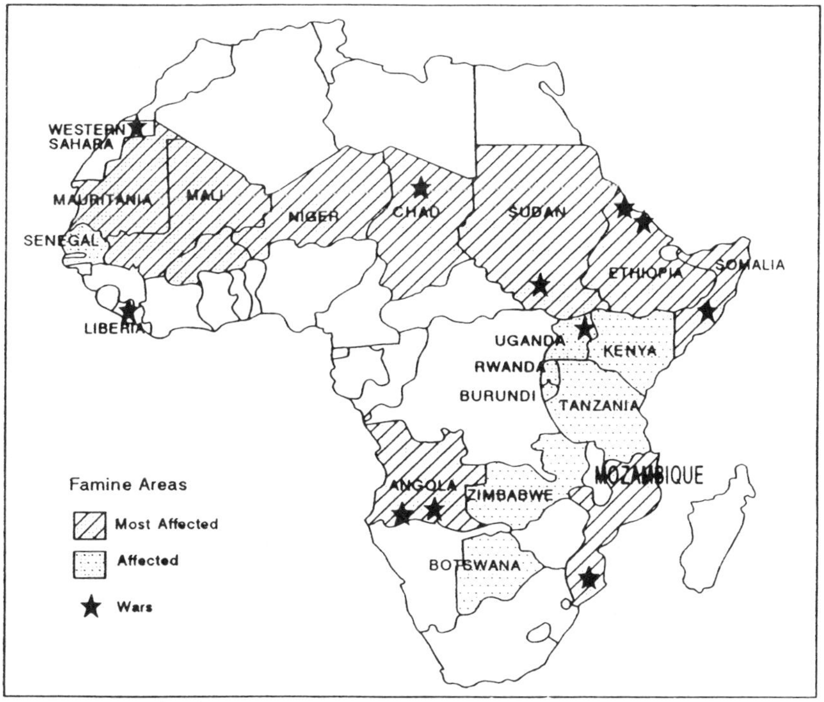


Figure 1.2. Famine areas and location of major wars in Africa, 1990. Source: M.E. Abu Sin (1990).

## Sudan Environment

Understanding Sudan's environmental ecosystem is an essential factor in understanding displacement processes. The country's colonial heritage and polarized development policies have been important elements in producing regional disparity, which in turn has generated population displacement. Economic dualism—composed of a modern, highly localized sector and a broad traditional sector—has created great anomalies in production systems and made Sudan vulnerable to environmental hazards that have generated displacement.

The following basic characteristics of the Sudan environment are central to understanding the causes and mechanism of displacement:

· There is wide ecological diversity in the natural physical environment.

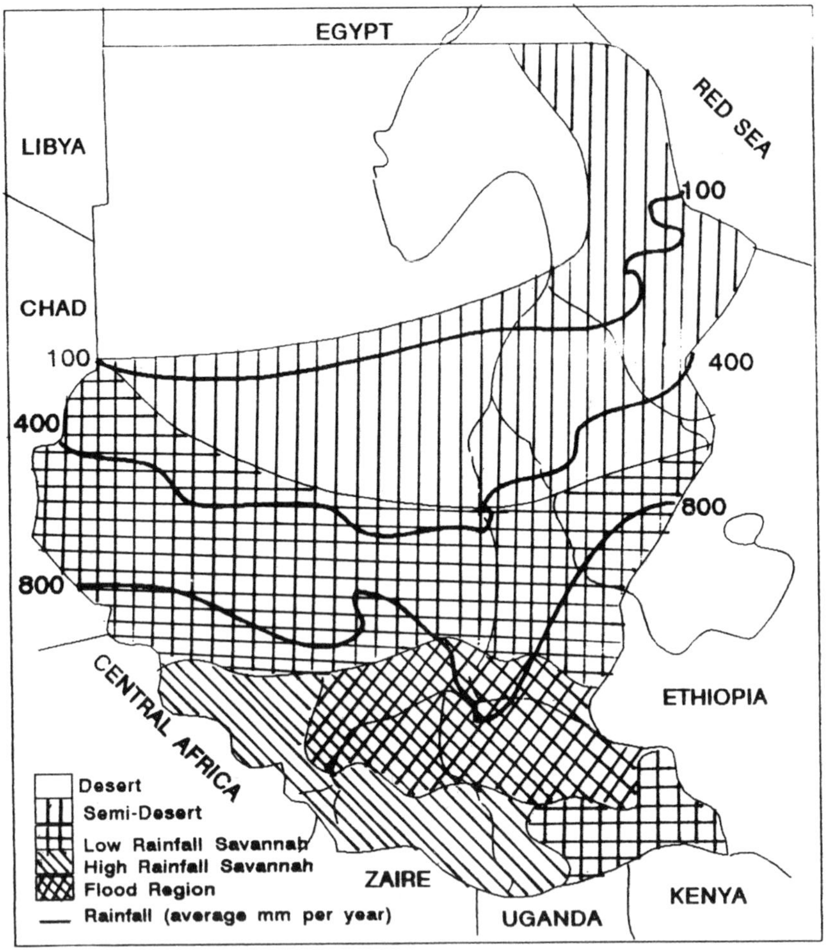


Figure 1.3. Ecological zones in Sudan. Source: M.E. Abu Sin (1990).

· The resource base has certain capabilities related to soil, landscape, hydrology, climate, geological structure, and natural biomass (fig. 1.3).

· The Nile River cuts across the ecological zones that house all the population engaged in the vulnerable traditional sector. Because of its valuable water and soil resources, it also accommodates modern-sector activities and is the refuge of the surplus population discharged from the traditional sector.

· The traditional sector, which supports more than 70 percent of the population, must scratch at meager and degraded natural resources; hence, it is rapidly losing its means of sustainability, a process accelerated by excessive drought conditions, low technological input, and so on (table 1.1).

Table 1.1. Sudan's Environment and Ecosystem

| Variable | Description |
|---|---|
| Area | 2.5 million square kilometers, extending longitudinally to 22.5 degrees north latitude, from true desert to an equatorial ecosystem. Desert and semidesert is about one-third of total area. The savanna belt, another one-third, houses the bulk of the population and is the seat of most of the economic activity. |
| Hydrology | The Nile River system, crossing the country from south to north, is the area with the highest resource potential. |
| Geology | The basement complex is composed of box rocks. |
| Soil | About 64 percent is loam; about 36 percent is sandy and rocky. Arable soil is about 192 million acres. |
| Rainfall | Ranges from zero to 1,000 millimeters per year, with a variability of 25 to 45 percent in normal years. Characterized by high seasonality and a low degree of reliability in sustaining natural or cultivated plants. |
| Population | 10.3 million people in 1956, 22.5 million in 1983, and about 25 million in 1993. Characterized by a high degree of feralism and a variety of ethnicities and cultures. More than 70 percent of the people are peasant farmers or nomads. That group, the traditional sector of the economy, is subject to greater environmental hazards and is at greater risk for concentration and displacement than the modern sector (figures 1.4, 1.5). |
| Economy | Composed of contrasting traditional and modern sectors with minimal linkage. Development has been intensified in the modern sector (agriculture, agro-industry, and urban-based investment) at the expense of the traditional sector and has increased the traditional sector's vulnerability to environmental hazards and has decreased its sustainability. Investment feedback in the traditional sector is minimal: the sector has collapsed completely under the pressures of drought, desertification, and its own conservative production system. The polarization of development between traditional and modern is evident in the regional and spatial concentration of the main irrigation systems, which are controlled by the Nile system (table 1.2). |

## Direct Causes of Displacement

There has been no reliable, detailed assessment of the causes of displacement, due to the recency of the phenomenon and the variations in its causes. In general, however, displacement is associated with interrelated causes, including purely environmental reasons, the security and strategies of the affected population, and historical and cultural factors. For example, one strategy of the affected population has involved its movement to Khartoum, thus making the authorities aware of the conditions of the displaced population as well as giving the problem political dimensions.

Despite the diverse causes of displacement, the displaced population can be classified into the following categories:

- Environmentally displaced
- War displaced
- Environmental and war displaced
- Multiple causes

Classification depends on the origins of the displaced population. Those displaced from ecologically marginal areas in the north have been driven by purely environmental causes: drought, desertification, and the collapse of the production system. On the other hand, those displaced from the south have been primarily driven by severe war conditions, which have resulted in the complete collapse of the production system.

Although environmental and war-related causes have magnified the displacement problem, other causes have also subjected certain populations to the risk of displacement. One is the country's colonial heritage and its policy of closing off some areas from the rest of the country. (These areas include the south, Ingesina, and Nuba Mountains.) During the colonial period, development was aimed at the areas of highest potential. This strategy has been continuously pursued since Sudan's independence in 1956, resulting in sharp regional disparities and dualism in the economy. As a result, parts of Sudan now have a modernized economic sector based on irrigated and mechanized agriculture, agro-industry, and urban-based enterprises, while the areas with low sustainability and high environmental risk have generally retained traditional production systems. These traditional areas accommodate more than 70 percent of the population, 80 percent of the livestock, and all the nomads in the country. In contrast, the high-potential areas accommodate the modern sector, which is limited in size and productivity. The links between the modern and traditional sectors have remained extremely weak; the two compete for arable land, water, space, and accommodation of rural population. Therefore, the areas available for traditional peasant farming and pastoral nomadism are shrinking, leading to an increased intensity in the use of the scarce resources that support the rural population.

Environmental degradation due to natural factors or man-made practices is the immediate cause of much of the present displacement process. Loss of arable land, desert encroachment, frequent drought, and loss of biomass have rapidly challenged the resilience of the traditional sector; and the failure of the traditional production system has contributed to environmental and resource-base degradation. As a result, most traditional sector areas are affected by drought (fig. 1.4) and chronic food insecurity (fig. 1.5). In addition, the government's strategy has emphasized the production of cash crops in the traditional sector, hence accelerating the use of resources, challenging

Table 1.2. Distribution of Major Modern Irrigation Systems in Sudan

| System | Location | Area (in acres) |
|---|---|---|
| Gezira | central | 1,920 |
| Er Rahad | eastern/central | 288 |
| New Halfa | eastern | 429 |
| Blue Nile | central | 591 |
| White Nile | central | 595 |
| Es Suki | central | 86 |
| Kenana | central | 77 |
| Assalaya | central | 36 |
| Guneid | central | 77 |
| Sennar West | central | 31 |
| Abu Na'ama | central | 29 |
| Main Nile | northern | 16 |
| Mechanized farming | central/eastern/Kordofan | 7,680 |
| Total | | 11,855 |

*Source:* Agricultural Bank of Sudan, *Annual Report* (Khartoum, 1989).

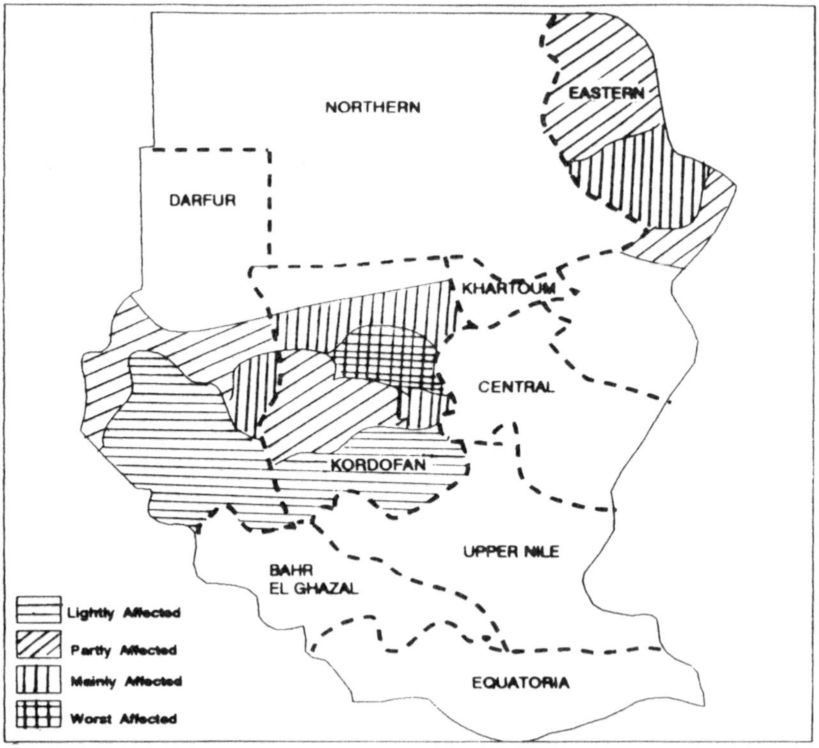


Figure 1.4. Drought-affected areas in Sudan, 1987. Source: M.E. Abu Sin (1990).

the food base of the traditional sector, and forcing a mass of people to move out of their traditional areas.

Uprooting the population causes cultural disturbances and family disintegration and shakes the social institutions. Displacement, on the other hand, blends the cultures of different communities. Empirical evidence suggests minimum cultural conflict among displaced populations from different cultural and ethnic backgrounds, perhaps due to common shared misery. Nevertheless, displacement disturbs fertility trends, sex and age structures, nutritional aspects, and the whole population setting. It also plays an important role in the ruralization of urban centers, and its impact on the demographic characteristics of rural or semiurban populations is evident from an observation of vital events and behavior.

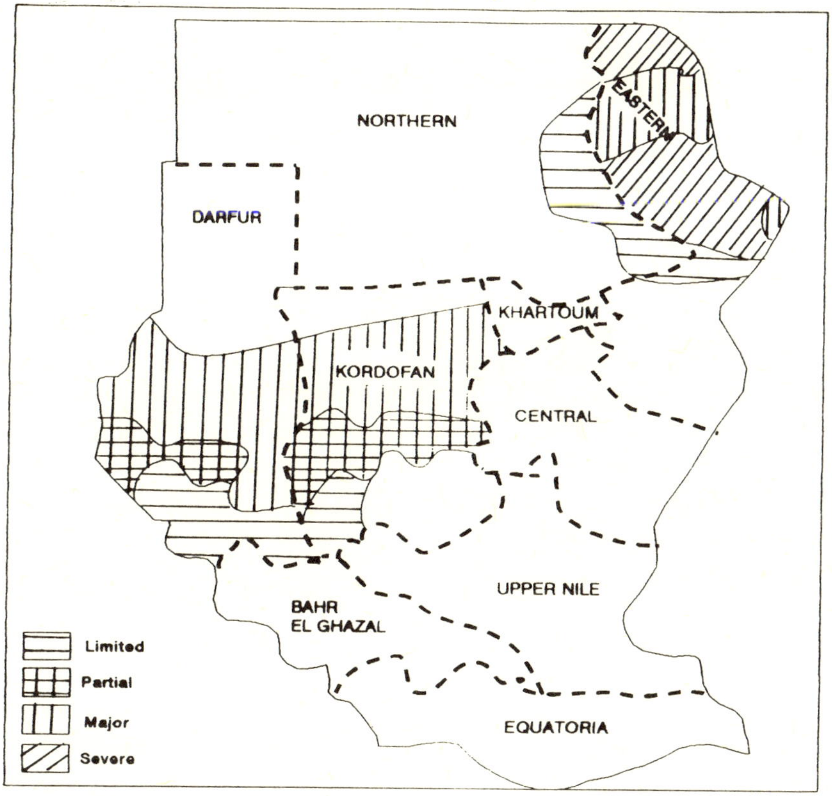


Figure 1.5. Areas of chronic food insecurity in Sudan. Source: M.E. Abu Sin (1990).

The war in the south is the most important single cause of displacement in terms of number of people involved and political dimension. It has contributed to displacement in three important ways: (1) by creating excessive northward movement among people from war areas, (2) by stopping economic activities in war areas, and (3) by displacing people from contact areas because of expected insecurity. The war's role in aggravating displacement reached its climax in the years 1985–90, causing over a million people to move north. Both the intensity of the war and its length of duration have increased the potential for displacement among people from the south.

An indirect yet influential factor in generating displacement is the relief policy of governmental and nongovernmental organizations

(NGOs). The concentration of relief centers in towns has been responsible for encouraging people to move to those centers instead of waiting in their home areas. The inefficiency of the infrastructure and the distribution system are the main causes for delay in the flow of relief into affected areas. Many rehabilitation programs have failed due to financial constraints and the security conditions in war-affected areas, thus adding to the lack of population stability in high-risk displacement areas.

## Environmental Impact of Displacement

As I have mentioned, detailed studies are needed to document and quantify the environmental impact of displacement. My aim in this chapter is limited to providing a framework for understanding and assessing the environmental impact and for guiding future research on the issue. With this goal in mind, I make the following general comments.

Population concentration in specific areas (particularly in large urban centers already suffering from congestion) and conditions that do not promote a sustainable way of life have affected public health, hygiene, nutrition, employment, and overall quality of life. Figure 1.6 shows the concentration of the displaced population in Sudan.

Among migrants, displacement causes psychological stress, increased submissiveness, and social and cultural detachment. For the homeland, displacement means the loss of human resources that might otherwise be mobilized for environmental protection, management, and monitoring to reverse the existing process of environmental degradation. Despite its complex and adverse environmental impact, however, displacement is producing pluralism and promoting social integration among various communities coexisting in recipient areas.

## Conclusion

The displacement of rural people and the resulting population concentration in urban centers are becoming important issues in Sudan's population redistribution and economic development prospects. They are directly related to a vulnerable environment, severe food shortages, development oriented toward maximum profit, war conditions, and the lack of sound resource management. In a country with a

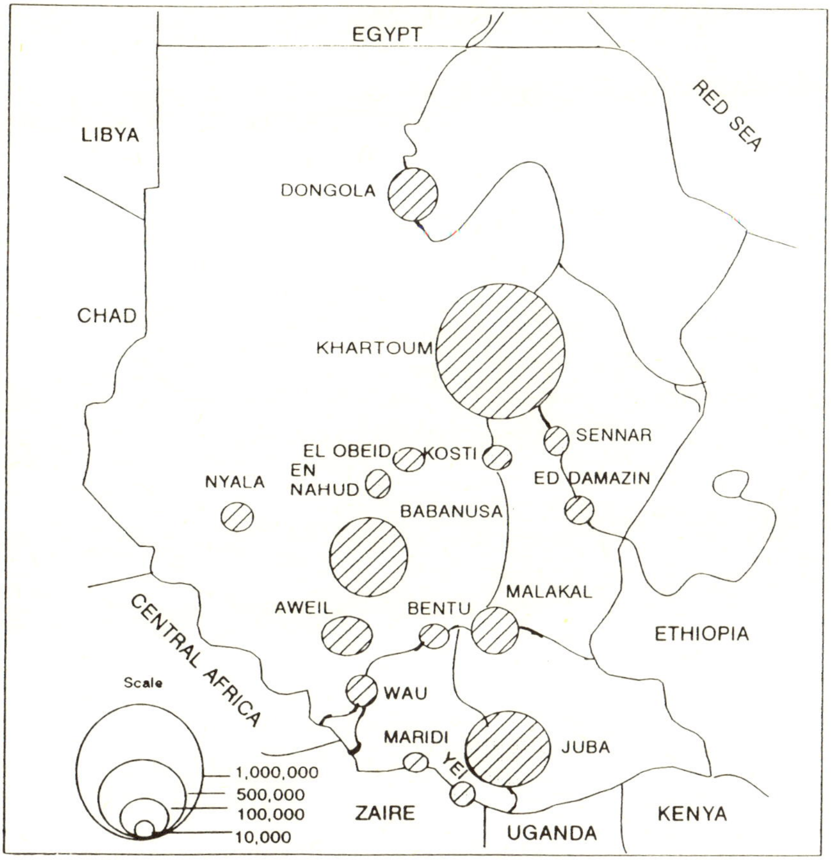


Figure 1.6. Receiving areas for displaced population in Sudan, 1990. Source: M.E. Abu Sin (1990).

stagnant economy, the large number of displaced people must soon assume top priority among planners and policymakers.

The need for policy guidelines to reverse the displacement trend is obvious, but they are difficult to implement. A clear population policy accompanied by necessary legislation and freedom of action appears to be the only answer. Such a policy must be an integral part of a national socioeconomic and political framework that also attempts to put an end to the war in the south and devise a flexible, objective approach to management aims and procedures. Within such a framework, the displacement issue might be approached in the following ways:

· Rehabilitate areas of emigration by implementing sustainable development projects compatible with the resource base of the community. Such projects should incorporate both environmental protection and development objectives. Small-scale, integrated projects could be the answer if they include community members as full participants and beneficiaries.
· Divert the displaced population into relevant and purposefully designed projects, preferably in purposefully developed areas.
· As a precondition for sustainable development, reverse and revise the old development strategy to satisfy the food security issues raised by the present government. Self-dependence should be the goal for both the government and the community.

The long-standing governmental policy concerning the displaced has been geared primarily toward providing relief and expelling the displaced from destination areas. This approach has proved to be ineffective; therefore, the logical option is a policy based on efforts related to origin, destination, and the displaced themselves.

Chapter 2

# Displacement and Migration As a Consequence of Development Policies in Sudan

*Hassaballa O. Hassaballa and Eltigani E. Eltigani*

In precolonial Africa, people moved from one place to another at a slow rate, usually because of epidemic diseases, starvation, drought, or war between tribal groups. The indigenous populations of the continent lived in tribal territories, making short or circular movements as their subsistence strategies demanded or as emergencies required.

In the traditional societies of Sudan, all socioeconomic activities were carried out by family members, who worked on a continuous annual cycle as pastoralists and agriculturalists. Production resources and relationships were organized to serve and satisfy the family needs and to strengthen the bonds of the tribal society. Although the resources for production—in particular, land, pastures, water, and other natural resources—were communally owned, they were entrusted to the tribal chief, who allocated the land resources among the community members and settled any disputes over the use of land and other natural resources. The tribal chief, however, had no authority to evict a tribesman from the land nor the right to allocate any plot of land to a relative or a family member without the consent of his subjects. The chief's responsibility was to regulate the use of tribal land with the free consent of his fellow tribesmen.

Within traditional societies, which were organized to achieve self-sufficiency in a system with limited cash transactions and a minimal market economy, the production relationship was based on ties of kinship and affinity. When there is an absence of economic exchange, land and produce are not transformed into value.[1] Therefore, traditional societies developed a system of prestations, counterprestations, redistributions, and generalized reciprocity to deal with food shortages and to support group self-sufficiency and welfare.

## The Colonial Mode of Production

When British colonists invaded Sudan in 1898, they imposed a new mode of production: the exploitation of local resources and the native population to serve colonial interests. Under the colonial mode of production, development policies concentrated on building railways, organizing large-scale irrigation schemes for cash crops (mainly long-staple cotton for export), and opening up new territories. In addition to expropriating land for these purposes, the colonial government imposed several taxes, including the personal tax (*Dignniya*), the hut tax (*Atab*), and the livestock tax (*Quta'an*). Furthermore, it opened the local market to foreign imports, mainly consumer goods. These policies were designed to establish and consolidate the country's colonial mode of production and to weaken the self-sufficient tribal populations and their traditional mode of production.

Traditional Sudanese societies were caught off guard by the new colonial production policies. Although many people became landless, they simultaneously had to pay taxes to the colonial authorities. In such a situation people had the choice of engaging in cash-crop production; selling their livestock; or migrating to earn cash for subsistence, to pay taxes, or to buy other market goods. Because large numbers of tribal people had become landless or had been driven into marginal land, it was very difficult for them to produce cash crops. Selling livestock for cash is a practice that nomads and pastoralists disdain because it goes against their sociocultural norms. Therefore, tribal people started to sell their own labor, often at construction sites or on large-scale agricultural schemes. Eventually, the bulk of the rural population came to believe that looking for wages meant engaging in labor migration. Thus, labor migration to agricultural schemes and to urban centers has increased rapidly over time.

## The Gezira Scheme

The Gezira scheme demonstrates how the colonial mode of production has transformed rural life and created a sizable population flow.

The scheme is situated in a triangle of land south of Khartoum. Two sides of the triangle are formed by rivers: to the east is the Blue Nile; to the west, the White Nile. The total area of the Gezira region is about five million acres, and the scheme itself occupies about 2.1 million acres.

The Gezira scheme was established in 1925 to provide long-staple cotton for textile factories in Lancashire, Great Britain. Other crops were also introduced during various stages of scheme development, including sorghum, wheat, groundnut, lubia, and rice. Today the scheme is the largest irrigated project in all of sub-Saharan Africa.

The impact of the Gezira scheme on the socioeconomic and political structure of the region can be evaluated by considering the production relationships among the different parties concerned in the scheme's operation. Its organization has often been described as a three-way partnership involving the government, which has supplied the main part of the infrastructure; the Sudan Plantation Syndicate (known as the Sudan Gezira Board after the scheme was nationalized in the 1950s), which manages the scheme; and the many thousands of tenant farmers who carry out the main part of the agricultural operations.

The production relationship introduced by the Gezira scheme was alien to inhabitants of the area. Before the scheme's establishment, most of the people led a seminomadic life. During the dry season they moved from one place to another in search of water and grazing land for their cattle. During the rainy season they lived in their villages and cultivated sorghum on the land around them. Economic production was organized in terms of lineage and the tribe. Within this system of economic organization, land was not a commodity because it was communally owned. Although it was frequently vested in one man or in one family, the land was held in trust for the entire group.[2] When the Gezira scheme changed the social organization of the irrigated area, social classes started to develop. These classes did not, of course, develop spontaneously. Their development was a result of preexisting social forces and social configurations within the particular structural opportunities produced by the scheme.[3]

Essentially, the land within the Gezira scheme is owned by the government, although the government formally leases it at an annual rental of ten piasters per 1.04 acre from those able to document ownership claims.[4] The way in which the land was taken over and the tenancies distributed has preserved some of the social and economic inequalities in existence before the scheme's establishment. Large landowners (mostly tribal and religious leaders) were able to obtain significantly larger shares in the scheme than were small landowners or those without land. When land was registered before the scheme was opened, many tribal and village leaders listed communally owned lands as their own private property, thus establishing ownership rights over land that was not theirs. In turn, the colonial government believed that allowing existing leaders to maintain some economic preeminence in the Gezira area was a political necessity. Because the government feared that these leaders might mobilize their people against the scheme, it tried to ensure support by giving leaders some stake in the project.[5]

An individual able to present a documented claim to forty acres or more is entitled to at least one tenancy of forty acres. If he claims seventy-seven acres or more, he is entitled to two tenancies. Such individuals are known as *right tenants*. If a right tenant owns 120 acres or more, he is entitled to name an heir, who is also given a tenancy. Such tenants are known as *nominees*. By nominating his close associates, a large landowner can be assured that 240 acres of irrigated land stays under his control or under the control of those close to him. The needs of others are considered only after the needs of the right tenants have been satisfied. *Preferential tenants* are those who own less than forty acres. Provided there is sufficient land available in the relevant locality, they can be granted a tenancy or a half-tenancy (nineteen acres). If tenancies still remain after the preferential tenants have been satisfied, the remaining plots (usually in half-tenancies) are given to landless cultivators or to outsiders.[6]

The technical conditions for successful cotton production have demanded the creation of an autonomous body called the Sudan Plantation Syndicate (now the Sudan Gezira Board), which ensures that the right inputs (labor, seed, fertilizer, water, and so on) are applied at the right time in the right sequence. Regimentation and control is inevitable; and in return for expected benefits, the tenants have to subordinate themselves. What, how, and when to grow are decisions beyond tenant control.[7] Thus, the role of a tenant on the Gezira scheme is in many ways close to that of a factory worker.

According to the scheme's system of production, the tenant and his family are responsible for the labor on the tenancy. The only recognized exception to this rule is during the peak seasons (sowing and cotton picking). Nevertheless, tenants routinely depend on hired labor, a situation necessitated by the fact that incomes from the tenancies are relatively low and unstable when compared with income from off-farm activities. The attractions of off-farm income have made it worthwhile for some tenants and their families to rely on these sources while at the same time hiring labor. In fact, a study by Abdel Salam revealed that during the 1975–76 season, the net income from off-farm sources amounted to 59.8 percent of the total net income of the tenants.[8]

At first, the Gezira scheme's main source of hired labor came from western and central Africa. Foreign migration to Sudan began at the turn of the twentieth century, a time when pilgrims crossed the country on their way to Mecca. During the trip they worked along the way to support themselves and to pay for their journey. After the scheme was established, the number of transient workers started to swell. Because the Gezira area lies close to the belt of immigration, tens of thousands of people flowed there either as settlers or as itinerant laborers.[9] This influx of western and central Africans was encouraged by the colonial government, due partly to the belief that they were more efficient and productive than the native population. More important, however, the immigrants provided cheap labor, which benefited the scheme administration and ultimately the colonial government by facilitating the production of competitively priced cotton.

Today, even after the scheme's nationalization and Sudan's political independence, the policy of recruiting migrant labor has continued, although more emphasis is now placed on attracting migrants from western Sudan and discouraging the migration of foreign labor. The Sudan Gezira Board (SGB) spends thousands of pounds on recruiting campaigns, mainly during the cotton-picking season. Potential recruits are offered advance payments, one-way transportation to Gezira, and free lodging in huts provided by the tenants. Approximately three-quarters of the migrant workers have been brought in by the Cotton-Picking Recruitment Committees or the tenants themselves.[10] In short, the tenancies' low, unstable incomes have led the most talented, energetic, and educated people in the area to seek employment elsewhere, mainly in Sudan's urban centers or abroad; and cheap agricultural labor has poured in, mainly from more economically depressed parts of the country (particularly the west).

As a result of the Gezira scheme, Sudan has witnessed the following economic developments:

1. Large-scale irrigated agricultural projects have became dominant in Sudanese agricultural development programs, and most have imitated the organizational and production structures of the Gezira scheme.
2. Tribal land users, now a rural landless class, have been displaced because no plans were designed to accommodate them after their land was expropriated.
3. Cotton has dominated grain as the backbone of the economy, thus strengthening the link between the Sudanese economy and foreign interests.
4. The scheme has turned Sudan into an export-oriented country dependent on the production of long-staple cotton.
5. It has created a bureaucratic and administrative elite who not only share common interests with the colonialists, but also hold colonial development policies as sacred truth.
6. Concentration on export crops has put great pressure and practical constraints on the use of human and natural resources to produce food. In the long run, this has led to food shortages and famine and has triggered an unprecedented mass exodus from rural areas to urban centers.

## The Postindependence Era

When Sudan achieved independence in 1956, it inherited the colonial approach to development, which featured an export-oriented economy, large-scale irrigated projects, land expropriation, and migrant labor. In general, postcolonial development programs followed the colonial mode of production, even to the point of expanding into new regions. During the 1960s and 1970s, Sudan governments began to assign more land to both the public and private sectors for export-oriented cotton production. The Gezira scheme expanded into lands known as the Managil extension, and an additional 384,000 acres were irrigated in the Khashm el Girba scheme in eastern Sudan.

Along the Blue and White Niles, 1.34 million acres were irrigated; and new projects such as El Rahad and El Suki were established to concentrate on cotton production.

New mechanized schemes (also known as rain-fed agriculture) were opened at El Dali, El Muzmum, Agadi, and Garabin in the Blue Nile Province and at Habila in Kordofan, supplementing the older ones in Gadambiliyya and Gedaref. These schemes concentrate on producing sorghum, sesame, and groundnut; but in some areas, such as the Nuba Mountains, cotton has been introduced.

The breadbasket strategy promoted by President Nimeiri's government during the 1970s emphasized cash- and staple-crop production in Sudan's central clay lands. This strategy focused on boosting commercialized agriculture to increase exports of food to Arabia and Africa.

All these projects were established on land that was previously inhabited and cultivated by indigenous populations and used by different nomadic tribes during their annual migrations in search of water and grazing areas. Thus, the projects have not only deprived the indigenous peasants of their livelihood, but have also disrupted traditional routes of migration and denied nomads access to water and grazing sources.

A common feature of every development plan designed during and after the colonial period is its neglect and disregard for the rural population's subsistence. Over time, nomads and peasants have been pushed into poor marginal areas, and their rural mode of subsistence has been deformed and destroyed. An enormous number of local inhabitants have become landless agricultural laborers or have drifted to urban centers to look for wage work.

### The Kenana Sugar Company

The Kenana Sugar Company illustrates the impact of postcolonial development strategies on migration and population displacement in Sudan. Located 320 kilometers south of Khartoum, the scheme was implemented in 1975, and sugar production began during the 1980–81 season. The total size of the estate is 150,000 acres, 80,000 of which are planted in sugarcane. It is administered by the Kenana Sugar Company (KSC), which is owned jointly by the Sudan government, foreign shareholders, and private Sudanese shareholders.

According to a 1972 agreement, the government has agreed to lease KSC 150,000 acres of land at an annual rent of ten piasters per 1.04 acre—almost a free lease. Although KSC presently has a thirty-year lease, it will be allowed to renew for another twenty years when the current lease expires. The government has also permitted the company to clear the area without any duties, charges, or any obligations to the indigenous population—the Dar Muharib. In essence, the government has not only given away Dar Muharib land, but also destroyed this rural society's life and set the population streaming out of the Kenana region.

In 1976, when heavy earth-moving equipment began to transform the Kenana site, nomadic tribes (such as Sabaha, Nabaha, Sebaig, Khanferiyya, Masalamiyya, Kibayshab, Ahamda, Selaym, and Kenana) and peasant tribes (such as Barti, Mima, Dajo, Fur, Gimir, and Fallata) paid close attention. People from villages such as Sufeiya, El Gargaf, Hillat Musri, Fangoga, Omdabakir, and Nuri began wondering about the future: would the Kenana scheme take away their sorghum fields, pastures, village sites, and campsites? KSC authorities told the people that the new project would change their poor, harsh lives to prosperous ones; people would have jobs, hospitals, schools, and more. Nevertheless, the indigenous population remained skeptical, for there seemed to be no correlation between losing its means of subsistence and gaining a good life.

To ease local tensions, the government promised compensation to every person who cultivated land within the boundaries of the Kenana scheme and for every hut owned by a family. The people of the Kenana region believed such compensation would enable them to start a new life somewhere else and pay for the cost of adjustment. To their astonishment, however, each person who owned an acre of land was given seventy-five piasters, and anyone who owned a hut received ten piasters. In other words, a family of seven persons who owned three huts and ten acres was paid approximately L.S. 8 for all its sorghum fields, huts, and campsites.[11]

Bitter and frustrated, the local population saw its means of subsistence slipping away. A delegation of Dar Muharib sheikhs met with the KSC administration, which promised them job opportunities, a canal for livestock owners, and small plots of land for local subsistence crops. But as time has shown, these promises were false;

KSC simply wanted to reduce tensions and pacify the former users of the land.

In numerous ways the Kenana scheme has victimized the indigenous people. During the scheme's construction, the inhabitants of Sufeiya village were asked to leave their homes; the village site became pump station 2. Then the inhabitants of Hillat Musri village were asked to leave their homes because the village lay within the boundaries of the Kenana town site. The KSC authorities do not want nomads or peasants in the irrigated area of the project. As a result, 40,000 nomads have been displaced, and 35,000 peasants have been affected—driven into fragile marginal ecosystems susceptible to drought and desertification.

Paradoxically, while the scheme has proletarianized and displaced the indigenous Dar Muharib, it has also opened the door to migrant and immigrant workers. This approach runs counter to our view that sustainable rural development should be designed to improve the living standard of the low-income groups residing in rural areas and to make their development self-sustaining.[12]

The efforts of KSC to attract migrant labor are strikingly similar to the Sudan Gezira Board's. In 1980 KSC sent two agricultural supervisors from Kosti to Nyala (in western Sudan) and Wau (in southern Sudan). Their main task was to recruit laborers (in particular, cane cutters), and local authorities in Nyala and Wau agreed to help in recruitment. Interested laborers received an advance payment of L.S. 10, free meals, and free train tickets to Kenana. As a result, most cane cutters on the estate came from western or southern Sudan. This recruitment strategy was important in two ways: it prevented a labor shortage, and it attracted poor rural laborers who could not afford to pay for transportation to look for work.

KSC's policy of recruiting seasonal workers from their place of origin was abandoned after the first production season because workers poured into Kenana from all over the country. Annually, more than one hundred thousand people show up before the start of the production season in mid-October, giving KSC an enormous pool of potential workers. From this mass of people, the administration hires only eight thousand workers each season.

Cane cutters constitute about 50 percent of Kenana's seasonal workers. During the 1983–84 production season, 52.4 percent came from northern and southern Darfur, followed by 22.6 percent from southern Sudan (see table 2.1). The bulk of the cane cutters from western Sudan are Awlad el Fur, followed by Massalit, Bani Hussein, Gimir, and Tama. The majority of southern cane cutters are Dinka, Shilluk, Nuer, Baria, and Azande.

Eighty percent of the cane cutters are between the ages of twenty-six and thirty-five.[13] Most of these young migrants move between their village communities and Kenana. Those from western Sudan leave villages suffering from drought, desertification, and sporadic famine to find work and secure subsistence both for themselves and for the families left behind. When the production season is over, they buy grain and bring home cash for other family needs—for example, seed, which they buy in hopes that rain will come. Economic necessity, civil war, and famine have also forced the people of southern Sudan into this seasonal labor migration.

## Mass Exodus to Khartoum

Greater Khartoum (including Khartoum, Omdurman, and Khartoum North) receives most of the rural migrants. In a survey, Galal el Din

Table 2.1. Distribution of Cane Cutters in Kenana Sugar Company by Provice of Origin, 1985

| | Number of Cane Cutters | |
|---|---|---|
| Province | Number surveyed | % of total |
| White Nile | 37 | 10.3 |
| Northern and Southern Kordofan | 12 | 3.3 |
| Northern and Southern Dar Fur | 188 | 52.4 |
| Upper Nile | 32 | 8.9 |
| Equatoria | 13 | 3.6 |
| Bahr el Ghazal | 36 | 10.1 |
| Gezira and Khartoum | 31 | 8.6 |
| Nile and Northern | 9 | 2.5 |
| Eastern, Red Sea, and Kassala | 1 | 0.3 |
| Total | 359 | 100 |

*Source:* H. O. Hassaballa, "Social Change and Society Transformation in the White Nile Province: The Kenana Project" (Ph.D. diss., University of Washington, 1986).

found that 40 percent of the greater Khartoum population consisted of migrants from rural areas.[14] His survey also showed that 73 percent of the migrants came directly from their place of origin, while 27 percent worked in agricultural schemes before coming to Khartoum. The number of migrants entering Khartoum increased enormously during the 1980s due to drought and famine in western, eastern, and southern Sudan; the city's population swelled from seven hundred thousand in 1971 to 1.8 million in 1983. The mass migration between 1983 and 1990 resulted in a city population of four million.[15]

The rapid migration to greater Khartoum and other urban centers can be attributed to socioeconomic and environmental push factors in the sending areas. In addition, pull factors (such as commercial and industrial activities, social services, and educational and government institutions) attract migrants to urban receiving areas. Despite the many determinants responsible for the unprecedented population explosion in Khartoum, the policy of expropriating land and displacing the rural people remains one of the most important. Once rural societies became landless and are forcibly driven from their region, they move to Khartoum or are pushed into poor marginal lands. During the drought of 1983–85, the rural societies that had been pushed into fragile ecosystems were the first to starve. As quickly as possible, they moved to the national capital seeking food and shelter and trying to draw attention to their plight.

## Conclusion

In precolonial Sudan, pastoralists and shifting agriculturalists controlled their means of production. Access to and use of the land was guaranteed to all members of tribal communities. By regulating their land use in long-term cycles, they allowed large fallow areas to regain fertility or be reforested. In this way, tribal societies not only preserved a human-environment equilibrium, but also maintained strategies of self-sufficiency.

The goal of the colonialists was to tap Sudan's natural and human resources for the benefit of the colonizing country. In the process, the human-land equilibrium and the tribal policy of self-sufficiency were destroyed in favor of the new cash economy. When large areas used by tribal communities were confiscated and taxes imposed on inhabitants, the indigenous population had no alternative except to migrate for wage work.

The colonialists imposed a development design characterized by an export-oriented economy, large-scale irrigated projects, land expropriation, migrant labor, and poor wages. After Sudan's independence, many policymakers followed the lead of their colonial predecessors when they designed new development strategies. These plans, which were initiated in the 1950s, have caused severe deterioration of agricultural production accompanied by a collapsing economy, all of which holds little promise for a rapidly growing population.

The colonial and postcolonial programs for developing an export-oriented economy have created social, political, and economic catastrophes. Their main result is the massive displacement of the rural population and an unprecedented mass influx of rural migrants into large-scale agricultural schemes and urban areas—in particular, Khartoum, which has been battered and devastated by the flood of the displaced.

Chapter 3

# War Displacement: The Sociocultural Dimension

*Salah El-Din El Shazali Ibrahim*

Discourse about displacement in Sudan, as well as population movements in general, seems limited either to spatial or economic perspectives.[1] Scholars tend to conceive of displacement as a form of geographic mobility (albeit forced) and therefore emphasize the number of displaced people, the direction of their movement, and their impact on receiving areas (including pressure on services and the impact on the labor market). Other contributions, for the most part impressionistic surveys by NGOs, contemplate interventions among the displaced. They focus on issues of nutrition, health, employment, housing conditions, and other manifestations of suffering.

Very little attention has been accorded to displacement as a social process that transforms existence, and its sociocultural dimension has also been grossly overlooked. This chapter addresses those concerns as they refer specifically to the southern Sudanese displaced by the civil war. I want to stress, however, that my primary objective is to draw attention to aspects of the sociocultural dimension of displacement rather than present results of research on displacement. By synthesizing secondary sources, the chapter attempts to construct a conceptual framework to guide subsequent research.

The chapter does not seek to analyze the causes of the civil war in Sudan, nor does it attempt to present a comprehensive assessment of the cost and impact of that war. I do not intend to trivialize the human cost or the economic impact of war; rather, I use this chapter to consider the war as a catalyst of socioeconomic and cultural change. My underlying assumption is that the processes of sociocultural change currently operating among the war displaced have been largely overlooked. If these processes are not counteracted soon, they may create serious problems for both the displaced (as individuals and as a community) and the larger society.

The chapter is divided into four sections. The first introduces the war-displaced community in Sudan. The second conceptualizes displacement as a socioeconomic process (in contrast to the spatial concept pervading the literature). The third illustrates the sociocultural dimension of displacement, and the fourth discusses the implications of sociocultural displacement and outlines some ways to mitigate its negative impact.

## The War Displaced in Sudan

The civil war in Sudan has destabilized the population in ways that have drastically affected the demographic structure of most Sudanese regions. If the war continues, this process of destabilization promises to depopulate the combat zones thoroughly; already, the population of those zones has found itself displaced.

The southern Sudanese are most affected by war displacement, and the majority have sought refuge at safer places within and outside Sudan. When war extended to areas outside the south, increasing numbers of Sudanese from other regions, particularly from the northern provinces of South Kordofan, South Darfur, and Blue Nile, found themselves facing displacement.

According to one official estimate, about 350,000 Sudanese have sought refuge outside the country because of the war.[2] These refugees, who represent about 8.5 percent of all the refugees in Africa, have fled to three main countries: Ethiopia (with 330,124 refugees), Uganda (with 10,000) and Kenya (with 1,300). Other sources give higher estimates. Very little is known about the conditions of these refugees except that they struggle with hardships common to African refugees in general.

The number of those displaced outside Sudan is only a trickle when compared to the magnitude of displacement within the country. It is generally agreed that the number of internally displaced people is substantial. Different sources present conflicting estimates of the number of displaced persons and their regional distribution.

According to one set of official figures, however, more than six million people were displaced in Sudan in 1989 (see table 3.1).

The National Dialogue Conference (1989) and UN sources give different estimates of the total number of displaced Sudanese and their regional distribution. According to the National Dialogue Conference, greater Khartoum accommodates three million displaced persons. UN sources estimate that 1.25 million live in Khartoum, twenty-five thousand live in each of the southern garrison towns and the transitional zones, and 1.45 million live in southern rural areas. MSF Holland (1988) maintains that the number of displaced persons in Khartoum ranges from one to two million.

Various factors underlie this disagreement over estimates, especially regarding regional distribution of the displaced. One major factor is that the conflicting estimates relate to different points in time; the intervening periods simply reveal fluctuations in both the numbers and their regional distribution. Another factor involves implicit strategies relating to practical issues, such as regional allocation of relief supplies. In addition, disagreement is also related to definitional differences. While UN sources focus on the number of southern Sudanese, government estimates include war-displaced people from western

Table 3.1. Regional Distribution of War-Displaced Sudanese, 1989 (in millions)

| | Reason for Displacement | | |
|---|---|---|---|
| Region | Security | Drought | Total |
| Northern | 0.08 | 0.08 | 0.16 |
| Khartoum | 1.80 | — | 1.80 |
| Central | 0.32 | 0.20 | 0.52 |
| Eastern | — | 0.60 | 0.60 |
| Darfur | 0.06 | 0.80 | 0.86 |
| Kordofan | 0.07 | 1.00 | 1.07 |
| Bahr Elghazal | 0.41 | — | 0.41 |
| Equatoria | 0.80 | — | 0.80 |
| Upper Nile | 0.56 | — | 0.56 |
| Total | 4.10 | 2.68 | 6.78 |

*Source:* Commissions for Displaced and Relief and Rehabilitation (Khartoum).

Sudan (southern Kordofan and southern Darfur) and the southeast (Blue Nile Province).

## Displacement As a Socioeconomic Process

The issue of displacement is not simply a question of counting the people who left their places of origin. It is also, and more significantly, a socioeconomic process through which otherwise self-sufficient people become impoverished, vulnerable, and in need of external assistance. The overwhelming majority of Sudan's displaced have undergone this process of impoverishment. It is important to remember that this concept of displacement does not include everyone who is forced to move from one place to another. For example, the community members of Juba University were spatially displaced when the university was relocated to Khartoum, but none of those members has been socially displaced. Likewise, affluent groups such as businesspeople, professionals, and civil servants are not displaced in a social or sociological sense.

Most socially displaced people once lived within the traditional sector, which is dominated by small-scale, subsistence-oriented farming and pastoralism. Like small producers in other parts of Sudan, they were affected by the intensive commercialization that obstructed capital accumulation and inhibited the development of productive forces within traditional production systems. Although poverty was a way of life, they nevertheless had access to productive resources (mainly arable land and livestock) that helped to support them. When market-oriented production (such as cash crops and sale of animals) did not meet their cash needs, they supplemented their income with seasonal labor migration. After they were displaced from their homes, however, they were denied access to any resources; and finding alternative sources of livelihood became a top priority.

In essence, social displacement is a manifestation of proletarianization—in other words, of transforming small farmers and pastoralists (who do not produce wages) into potential wage workers divorced from the means of production. One immediate problem facing the displaced is finding employment and a relatively secure source of income, a process that varies among different categories of the displaced. For example, those displaced within southern Sudan, as well as those who end up in other rural regions, do not seem to experience social displacement to the same extent or in the same way as those who end up in large urban areas.

In the countryside, agricultural employment creates opportunity, but its seasonality poses severe problems. In that respect, urban areas are relatively better because they provide more kinds of nonseasonal employment. Some displaced men have established themselves as unskilled construction workers or have penetrated into service activities in the urban informal sector, but most are unemployed. Although the sheer size of the urban population has created many opportunities in the social and personal services sector, the sector itself recruits selectively among the displaced, providing far more opportunities for women than for men (for example, in domestic services, sale of beer and alcohol, and prostitution). This situation has affected customary gender roles: a majority of households have come to depend on female members as the sole breadwinners.

The general conditions of the people who fled from the war areas to safety do not seem significantly better than those of the people who remained in the war zone. In greater Khartoum, for example, the majority of the displaced squat in garbage dumps. One report describes the living conditions of these squatters:

> Housing [consists of] . . . make-shift card-board toukuls . . . built on garbage dumps on the outskirts of Khartoum. Amid broken glass, tin cans, plastic bags and general urban refuse, families have scraped small patches clean, built temporary shelters and crowd together. There is no running water, no latrine facilities, minimal health services, no electricity. Water is provided by donkey-carts at prices . . . [that make] it difficult to procure sufficient water. . . . Most of the people in the settlements live on the brink of existence with an irregular income, if any, with no legal right to settlement, with no identification papers from the authorities and thus without legal right to stay in Khartoum.[3]

All reports about these settlements voice concern over the deteriorating sanitary conditions. Some cases of severe diarrhea (similar to cholera) have been reported, but cholera itself has not been diagnosed.[4] A few NGOs, together with government departments and UNICEF, are providing services for the displaced in greater Khartoum, but more help is needed, particularly to improve sanitation.

The conditions of the displaced in other parts of the country, especially the south and the transition zone, are generally undocumented; however, they are probably as poor as Khartoum's, if not worse.

Children who attended schools in the combat zone form another category of the socially displaced. Because of war conditions, many schools in the region have been closed. Recent estimates by the Ministry of Education suggest that 84 percent of primary schools, 78 percent of intermediate schools, and 72 percent of secondary schools no longer provide education for southern Sudanese children, the generation that will control Sudan's future.[5] Simultaneously, massive numbers of students have fled into safer areas within and outside of the south. Officials estimate that one million children have been displaced, but the proportion of school-age children (those between ages 7 and 15) is unknown. Statistics from 1984 show that 413,350 students attended general educational institutions in southern Sudan, and at least two-thirds (275,567 students) may have been affected by school closures.

Due to capacity constraints in the receiving areas, most displaced students face enormous difficulties in finding room in schools and, in effect, have been denied access to education. The Ministry of Education has attempted to assess the number of displaced students outside the south, but those estimates indicate how little is actually known about student conditions (table 3.2).

The only available statistics concerning re-enrolled displaced pupils are for Khartoum, which estimates 15,730. The National Dialogue Report maintains that government-funded schools (including ten secondary, sixteen intermediate, and twenty-two primary) will open during the evening to absorb displaced pupils. Four nongovernment

Table 3.2. Distribution of Displaced Students Outside Southern Sudan, 1989

| Region Left | Region Entered | Number Displaced |
|---|---|---|
| Bahr El-Ghazal | Darfur | 22,000 |
| Bahr El-Ghazal and Upper Nile | Kordofan | 23,000 |
| South | Central | — |
| South | Khartoum | 15,730 |

*Source:* Ministry of Education (Khartoum, 1989), 35.

schools (three intermediates funded by the Catholic church and one primary funded by the Islamic Da'wa) also plan to open.[6]

The disruption of the educational system in war-torn areas has far-reaching implications for the future of affected students, families, and communities. Education is a major vehicle for social mobility in Sudan, particularly in the south. In general, educated Sudanese have better employment opportunities, which not only secure decent living conditions for themselves and their families, but also allow them to improve the condition of their communities (through education, health services, and so on). Notwithstanding the country's recent problems with educated unemployment (particularly in Khartoum), educated Sudanese generally face little difficulty in securing employment in the south, where opportunities are still available.

## The Sociocultural Dimension

Displacement has aroused mounting concern in Sudan. Much of it, however, stems from a negative conception of the displaced. They are generally considered a threat to health, security, and social order and responsible for the pressure on social services and the shortage of basic goods. Therefore, assessments of the impact of displacement tend to focus on how the displaced have contributed to the emergence or deepening of problems. The impact of displacement on the displaced themselves is generally trivialized or disregarded. Only their need for employment, food, and medical relief receives attention.

The impact of the civil war and displacement on social services and human welfare can be considered a short-term phenomenon. When the war ends, the government and others may renew efforts to rehabilitate the war-affected areas. Although the cost of rehabilitation will be expensive, external assistance can create changes within a relatively short period of time.

Nevertheless, displacement has long-term consequences that cannot be easily rectified. The disruption of the sociocultural organization of the affected communities, the intensification of intergroup conflict in the war zone, the psychological damage inflicted on those who survive the war, and environmental degradation are some of the long-term consequences that will linger long after the war is over and the infrastructure has been repaired. These consequences are rarely considered by either combatants or observers, partly because they are not readily visible events (such as increased crime or the emergence of squatter settlements) but gradual processes that take time to crystallize.

The most obvious disruption in the sociocultural organization of southern Sudan has been the uprooting of local communities and the disintegration of family structures.[7] Death due to war has dramatically increased the number of widows and orphans, and many family members are separated when they flee from the war zone or when men, willing or not, join the combat. Before displacement, widows and orphans were cared for by a male relative of the deceased, usually a brother. General destitution, however, has forced relatives to evade this customary obligation; as a result, most displaced households are headed by women. In a society in which authority over children is vested in the male head of the family (a father or a first-degree relative), a household headed by a woman exercises little authority over its children.

Because of such family disintegration, the number of street children in urban areas has reached alarming proportions. It is estimated that in greater Khartoum there are more than forty thousand children on the streets. Deprived of decent housing, a balanced diet, and education or training opportunities, street children are faced with a bleak future. There has been much speculation about the impact of deprivation on the attitude of these children toward society. Some believe that street children are criminals in the making; others think they are potential political agitators. No one, however, seems to dispute that they are victims not only of war but also of social negligence. Although a handful of national and international NGOs is working to rehabilitate them, the number of street children served by these interventions is very small. More must be done, and urgently.

Displacement has brought about sociocultural confusion because most displaced people can no longer uphold deep-rooted values, norms, and social institutions. The evasion of customary obligations to widows and orphans is an example of disintegration caused by impoverishment. In other cases, however, the confusion stems from sociocultural displacement. Loss of cultural traditions creates deep psychological distress among displaced people who are coping with the humiliating realities of their new life in diaspora. Reports have shown an increase in psychological and psychiatric disturbances among the displaced, which are caused at least partly by sociocultural displacement.

Sociocultural displacement is a process through which a community, due to external factors and contrary to its own will, is denied access to objects and symbols that are central to the maintenance and propagation of its sociocultural identity, value systems, and practices. One example is a displaced pastoralist's loss of his cattle. In this case, cattle are more than food or the means of production. They are also cultural symbols that mediate interactions relating to marriages, rituals, settlement of disputes—where killing is involved—and status. Now that many displaced pastoralists have lost their cattle, they often cannot accept the alternatives. Some of these alternatives are culturally stigmatized; in other words, they directly contradict everything cattle stood for in the home area. This is particularly true of using cash rather than cattle to pay bride wealth or as compensation for violations against chastity. According to the culture, cash payments do not define a relationship as marriage or legitimize the offspring of such a relationship. Instead, one makes cash payments to hire prostitutes.

Sociocultural displacement has put a considerable burden on married women, particularly those whose bride wealth was paid in cattle. Under normal conditions, conjugal conflicts resulting in divorce meant repaying the bride-wealth cattle to the husband. In diaspora, however, no cattle are available. Therefore, the relatives of wives subject the women to extreme pressure, urging them to put up with husbands to avoid divorce. Thus, a wife living unhappily with an unemployed husband must work harder to earn extra income, which she then must turn over to her husband.

Sociocultural displacement is not necessarily a corollary of spatial or social displacement; it may also be experienced by groups still living in the south. For example, some groups find it difficult to maintain the institution of the extended family due to their intensified fear of war conditions. One study has reported that "couples with small and noisy little children have been pushed away and forced to set up their homestead a considerable distance from the other members of the extended family and community."[8] People who keep livestock in communities where animal husbandry is not common have also been expelled. During the night, children and domestic animals tend to attract the attention of passersby, who may turn out to be soldiers searching for food or bandits looking for valuables. Many villagers fear that such attraction may result in indiscriminate shooting.

Manibe has capsulized the security concerns of civilians in the war zone and the way in which people respond to potential threats:

> The effect of security is seen in a practice evolved to cope with the behavior of a domestic animal—the cock. A contraption made of a thin rubber band has been devised and is put round the neck of a cock to prevent it from crowing loudly. The sight of cocks wearing these contraptions might be amusing but the security concerns of the people are real.[9]

Security concerns in the war zone indicate deep psychological distress among the civilian population. This distress does not result simply from the anticipation of future calamity; it is also a consequence of past experience. Virtually everyone in the combat zone has been personally affected by the tragedies of the war. Many have watched loved ones die in pain from bullet wounds, burns, or mutilation. These agonizing images of the past haunt the population at least as much as the prospect of another raid.

The flight from the war zone has increased psychological damage among the displaced. Separation from relatives, loss of belongings, and uncertainty about present and future add to the pressure. The registers of psychiatric hospitals and clinics note an escalation in psychological and psychiatric disorders among southern Sudanese living in camps around Khartoum. Most common is schizophrenia (60 percent), followed by depression and alcohol addiction.[10]

The war in Sudan has killed many people, but it has also destroyed the lives of survivors by inflicting deep psychological wounds. Unfortunately, it shows no sign of ceasing: war lines have extended to areas outside the south, and the conflict now involves new groups. In the process, human, sociocultural, and economic costs of war continue to mount.

## Conclusion

In drawing attention to aspects of sociocultural displacement, I want to stress that I am not idealizing the socioeconomic organization or sociocultural premises of displaced communities. Certain aspects of these communities have long shown a disregard for human rights, equity considerations, and the environment. In addition, the social order, including the sociocultural dimension, was in the process of change before displacement: commercialization processes were rapidly intensifying small-scale agriculture and pastoralism; commodification of labor through generalized wage relations (often in the form of seasonal labor migration) was introducing new social production relations; and new forms of social differentiation were emerging when the traditional leadership was challenged by a new generation of educated elite.

These processes depended on the preexisting social order (including prevalent forms of production, social institutions, power relations, and values and norms) to introduce change gradually. Now, however, the displaced have experienced a qualitatively different dynamic and logic for social change. A state of virtual anomie (the disintegration of norms) in its classic Durkheimian sense seems to prevail among the displaced, and there is a high degree of uncertainty and helplessness influencing the pace and direction of change.

The characterization of sociocultural displacement as a condition of disintegration does not imply that the displaced are unable to give meaning to their existence and suffering. Nevertheless, their coping responses mask uncertainty, anxiety, and stress; the most important social control mechanism is not internalized values and norms but the threat of the superior power (be it the government or members of other groups).[11]

The rapid social change experienced by the displaced is becoming a process of alienation—of abstraction from cultural roots that give symbolic meaning to existence and exercise social control and interaction. Undoubtedly such an abstraction has social revolutionary potential; but without conducive socioeconomic conditions, the consequences may instead be antirevolutionary and counterproductive.

Social revolutionary potential looms in the proletarianization of the people and the undermining of tribal values and social organization. Arabic and Islamic influence has increased among southern Sudanese displaced in the north, which may have a positive impact on nation-building initiatives by fostering social and cultural interaction between northern and southern Sudanese. In the history of Western Europe, analogous assimilation processes have contributed to industrial revolution and the emergence of the modern nation-state. Still, events in war-torn Sudan cannot be legitimately construed as an enactment or reiteration of that historical process.

During a mounting economic crisis, the proletarianized labor force is largely redundant in a stagnant, saturated labor market; therefore, relief must be perpetually extended to the displaced. As long-term relief becomes untenable (relief, by definition, is intended to be temporary and short-term), the revolutionary potential of proletarianization may become a destructive physical force. Presumably Sudan authorities have a clear understanding of this potential for destruction when they seek to evacuate the displaced from large cities.

Averting the destructive potential of displacement requires a strategy that entails more than evacuation. First, peace conditions must prevail in order to curb the war's drain on resources, which must then be rerouted to the rehabilitation of the war displaced. Second, the strategy for rehabilitation should consider Sudan's socioeconomic reality. Because small producers in regions far from the combat zone are consistently being marginalized and displaced, we cannot assume that returning the war displaced to their original homes will stabilize the situation. The rehabilitation strategy must be sensitive to the processes operating in the Sudanese social formation and include a comprehensive plan to release the developmental potential of small producers. The plan should not necessarily be geared toward restoring the prewar social order; such an objective is unrealistic given the pace and extent of existing social change. Instead it needs to be based on the skills, resources, and potentials of small producers as well as on their consent and participation; it needs to make their benefit a primary objective. Such a course will make the development process itself a tool of peace. Other courses of action, particularly those based on Sudan's past approach to development planning, may prove irrelevant, unacceptable, and counterproductive. They may also exacerbate grievances and perpetuate civil war in the south or other regions and intensify further sociocultural displacement.

Chapter 4

# Education of Displaced Southern Students in Northern Sudan

*Stephen A. Wol*

Before 1983 the southern Sudan government's Ministry of Education annually sent three hundred bright southern students to Khartoum's secondary schools and teacher-training institutes. The government had two aims behind this policy: to instill students with a feeling of national unity and to educate future teachers of Arabic. But as a result of the civil war in the south, which broke out in 1983, thousands of students lost not only their parents and homes but also their chance for an education. Consequently, large numbers of school children, with or without their parents, traveled to northern Sudan in search of security, shelter, food, and educational opportunities.

## Displaced Students in Northern Schools

When the southern government sent students to northern schools, it based its selection on the results of the intermediate final examination. Those students who scored highest were accepted. After the south was divided into three regions and the civil war began, student migration to the north increased tremendously. At first, most of the student migrants were from Bahr El Ghazal and the Upper Nile regions, where rebel activity was intense. As soon as they arrived in Khartoum, the central Ministry of Education and Instruction registered them and distributed them throughout northern secondary schools and institutes of education.

In 1985 the influx of students into the north increased so much that 450 students from Bahr El Ghazal and Upper Nile could not find places in northern schools. In response, the government opened a special school for them at Rufaa (Sheikh Lutfi Secondary School). During the 1986–87 academic year, the number of displaced students who could not find places in northern schools continued to grow, and more secondary schools were opened for them (Maridi in Khartoum and Imatong in Omdurman).

By the beginning of the 1990–91 academic year, there were ten special secondary schools for displaced southern students (not including the school at Rufaa). The following list identifies school names and locations: Maridi Girls, Khartoum; Maridi Boys, Khartoum; Owingibul Boys, Khartoum; Owingibul Girls, Khartoum; Sobat Girls, Khartoum; Wau Technical, Khartoum; Imatong Mixed, Omdurman; Shambe Mixed, Omdurman; Fashoda Boys, Khartoum North; and Tonj Girls, Khartoum North. All these secondary schools operate in the afternoon (except for one morning school) because the owners of the buildings use them at other times of the day. Out of the ten schools, only four actually operate on government school premises (Maridi Girls, Maridi Boys, Imatong Mixed, and Wau Technical). The rest function in hired private schools.

Displaced intermediate and primary pupils were absorbed into northern schools until the 1985–86 academic year. At that time, the education authorities of Bahr El Ghazal, with the cooperation of the governor and the director of the coordination office in Khartoum, opened six intermediate schools and nine primary schools. Although these schools were managed by personnel from Bahr El Ghazal and financed by the Bahr El Ghazal Region, the students were from the three southern regions. Bahr El Ghazal continued to run the schools until the end of the 1988–89 academic year.

## The National Committee to Organize Education of Displaced Students

The Council for the South, which was formed by the government of the Revolutionary Command Council for National Salvation, took a keen interest in the education of displaced southern students. After holding several preparatory meetings to identify problems, the supervisor general of the council asked the minister of education and instruction to meet in a joint effort to solve the educational dilemma. That meeting, which was held at the Ministry of Education and Instruction on 24 July 1989, organized an educational workshop to delve into the issue of displaced students from the south. On 14 September 1989 the workshop was convened. Following the recommendations of workshop participants, the Council of Ministers decreed that the National Committee should be formed to organize the education of displaced students (resolution 168, 28 September 1989).

By this time the number of displaced students in secondary schools had grown out of control, and the primary and intermediate schools needed to join the secondary schools under a unified administration. (Previously the primary and intermediate schools had been administered by the coordination offices of the regions.) With the inception of the National Committee, the three levels of general education could function smoothly under one umbrella.

## Schools, Students, Teachers, and Nonteaching Staff in the 1990–91 Academic Year

### Secondary Education

The following list shows the number of students absorbed into secondary schools in various northern regions: Central, 1,700; Northern, 615; Eastern, 500; Kordofan, 102; Darfur, 50; and Khartoum, 513. In addition, 636 students attended technical schools and 295 attended institutes of education, making a total of 4,416 displaced secondary students educated in the north.

In greater Khartoum, ten special schools were opened for displaced secondary students. The following list breaks down the total number of students by school: Maridi Girls, 794; Maridi Boys; 1,260; Owingibul Boys, 590; Owingibul Girls, 619; Sobat Girls, 640; Wau Technical, 144; Imatong Mixed, 810; Shambe Mixed, 840; Fashoda Boys, 870; Tonj Girls, 749; with a total of 7,316 students.

In 1990–91 there were 590 teachers, 40 classified staff members, and 116 unclassified staff members working in the ten special secondary schools for displaced students, making a staff total of 746.

### Intermediate Education

In 1990–91 there were eighteen intermediate schools for displaced pupils operating in greater Khartoum, with a total enrollment of 8,379 students. Khartoum had eight schools; Khartoum North, six; and Omdurman, four. In the eighteen intermediate schools, there were 108 teachers and 60 members of the support staff, with a staff total of 168.

### Primary Education

In greater Khartoum there were thirty-five primary schools for 19,016 displaced students, distributed as follows: Khartoum, sixteen schools; Khartoum North, nine; and Omdurman, ten. These schools employed 165 teachers and 83 members of the support staff, with a staff total of 248.

It is important to remember, however, that students throughout various regions of the north (mainly Darfur, Kordofan, Central, and Eastern) have no opportunity for education.

## Financial Support for Schools for Displaced Students

The education of displaced students is primarily funded by the central government, the southern regional governments, and grants offered by organizations and friendly countries. Money for students who have been distributed into regional schools is usually sent to the director general of education in each region. It is used to pay for food, school materials, uniforms, housing, and so on. At the end of each month, students who are studying in the special schools in greater Khartoum receive a stipend of L.S. 10 per day to meet the costs of transport and food. Although they also receive cash to pay for uniforms, their other requirements are provided by the school. Primary and intermediate students do not receive cash; instead, they are given school materials by their schools.

The salaries and wages of teachers and nonteaching staff are met by the regional governments. In addition, staff members also receive an additional 65 percent of their basic salaries to meet the costs of transport, housing, and so on. This second payment is made by the National Committee. A small number of teachers who receive their full salaries from the National Committee have been locally appointed by the committee to meet teaching shortages.

## Conclusion

It is worthwhile to say a few words about the difficulties that the National Committee has encountered. Although the Council of Ministers empowered the committee to control the educational policy for displaced students and to administer their primary, intermediate, and secondary schools, it still lacks the force to work effectively and efficiently. One reason relates to the sheer number of students in the schools. Originally, these schools were opened to educate southern students. Today, however, they also serve displaced students from other areas of Sudan. In addition, the committee has no funds to hire school buildings; build cheap classrooms for primary and intermediate students; buy office furniture, equipment, and stationery; or buy vehicles for transporting staff members, inspectors, and school supplies.

More effort should be made to provide financial support to the National Committee from the central government, international organizations, NGOs, and public donations. Providing educational opportunities to displaced southern students should be a priority of the central and regional governments so that a generation of southern children does not lose the chance to be educated. The importance of educating southern displaced students is derived from the fact that these students represent the future leaders of the south, on whose training and talents the development of the region rests.

Chapter 5

# Health Implications of Displacement in Sudan

*Eltigani E. Eltigani*

Over the past several years, Sudan's unprecedented displacement problem has meant that millions of people have been forced to leave their home areas. This movement was precipitated during the mid-1980s by drought in the eastern and western parts of the country as well as the civil war and armed conflict in the south and west. There are no reliable estimates of the number of people involved in this mass movement; however, most researchers believe that at least six million persons are involved and that Khartoum alone is host to at least two million, mainly from the south and west. Other parts of the country have also been affected.

The displacement problem has added to the already high rate of population mobility; it has been estimated that more than one million persons are on the move every year.[1] This continuous population flow has serious health implications for both the displaced people and the receiving areas. Because of poor environmental and sanitation conditions in slum areas, where most displaced people settle, they have become breeding grounds for communicable diseases. The impact of such diseases is not limited to the slums but has spread to the general population of cities and towns near the settlements. For example, diseases such as kala-azar and sleeping sickness have started to appear in Khartoum. Although the spread of disease has been attributed to the influx of displaced southerners, the displaced may also be exposed to diseases not prevalent in their own native areas.

In this chapter I identify the major health problems of the displaced as well as attempt to reveal the underlying reasons for these problems. As I discuss, such an understanding is important for those who design health programs and health delivery systems to combat the problems associated with displacement.

The data on which this study is based are collected from secondary sources, mainly the monthly reports submitted by relief organizations to the Commission of Health in Khartoum and the health unit of the Relief and Rehabilitation Commission (RRC). The reporting system, however, is not standardized; it differs among relief agencies and even among displaced settlements run by a single agency. This makes comparison of settlements difficult. There are also many gaps in the data, which add to the difficulty. In addition to using secondary sources, I made field visits to several displaced settlements in Khartoum. During all my visits, I conducted informal interviews with health personnel and inhabitants.

## Health Problems of Displacement

Thus far the term *health* has not been quantified for statistical purposes. Nevertheless, in its 1946 constitution, the World Health Organization (WHO) declared health to be a "state of complete physical, mental and social well-being and not merely the absence of disease or infirmity."[2] This concept of health emphasizes the importance of environmental, sanitary, psychological, and socioeconomic variables on health conditions. In the absence of a rigorous measurement of health, certain indicators are used as proxy measures, including mortality level of both adults and children, nutritional status of the population, morbidity level due to communicable and psychological diseases, and access to health services.

Sudan's displaced population is particularly vulnerable to various health problems due to the harsh environmental and socioeconomic conditions under which it lives. For the most part, people settle in squatter and slum settlements on the peripheries of towns and villages. Their dwellings are constructed of kenaf sacks, tents, cardboard, or straw. Basic amenities such as a safe water supply and sanitation services are not available in many slum settlements because local authorities want to discourage people from permanently settling in these areas. The lack of these basic amenities has an adverse impact on the general health conditions of the population. Unsafe water, for example, is associated with an increased incidence of mortality from communicable diseases, particularly diarrheal diseases.[3]

Most of the housing in the settlements is poorly built and unable to withstand changing weather conditions. In addition, housing materials often contribute to the spread of disease. For example, in Gezira the temporary straw houses used by migrant workers are a breeding ground for mosquitos, particularly during the peak cotton-picking season.[4] Each structure is crowded with residents, which contributes to the spread of infections (such as respiratory-tract infections), particularly among children.

To some extent, the adverse health conditions caused by poor environmental and sanitation conditions can be mitigated by appropriate health services. These services, including physical and social assistance, are an important factor in creating better health conditions for the displaced.

## Health Conditions of the Displaced

Malaria is the major health problem in all the settlements, followed by respiratory-tract infections and diarrheal diseases (table 5.1). Purulent conjunctivitis, skin diseases, wounds, and injuries are also prevalent. Most of the diseases are caused by poor sanitation and environmental conditions. Wounds and injuries are primarily due to violence associated with alcohol (a major source of income for many settlement residents) as well as increased stress and frustration created by the process of displacement and the living conditions in the settlements. According to the Omdurman Psychiatric and Psychologic Hospital, schizophrenia, alcohol addiction, and depression are extremely common. Almost 60 percent of the hospital's displaced patients have been diagnosed with schizophrenia, most of them between the ages of seventeen and thirty.[5]

The presence of malaria in a community is usually determined by a combination of environmental factors and the interaction between the human and mosquito populations, which fluctuates with seasonal patterns of temperature, humidity, and the availability of mosquito breeding sites. Today malaria is endemic in Sudan and plays a critical role in child survival. Pregnant women, infants, and young

Table 5.1. Malaria, Diarrhea, and Respiratory Tract Infection Cases as a Percentage of Total Outpatient Clinic Attendance in Selected Displaced Settlements, Khartoum, February-July 1990

| | Malaria | | | | | | Diarrhea | | | | | | Respiratory Tract Infections | | | | | |
|---|---|---|---|---|---|---|---|---|---|---|---|---|---|---|---|---|---|---|
| Settlement | Feb. | Mar. | Apr. | May | June | July | Feb. | Mar. | Apr. | May | June | July | Feb. | Mar. | Apr. | May | June | July |
| Hilat Shouk | 26.4 | — | — | 29.2 | 19.2 | — | 8.0 | — | — | 5.9 | 10.9 | — | 23.4 | — | — | 22.4 | 22.4 | — |
| Kalakla | 25.8 | — | — | 28.1 | 19.7 | — | 13.0 | — | — | 6.8 | 13.1 | — | 26.8 | — | — | 23.6 | 18.1 | — |
| Hilat Gadida | 22.1 | — | — | 22.3 | 30.3 | — | 15.2 | — | — | 8.1 | 10.8 | — | 22.5 | — | — | 18.6 | 10.4 | — |
| Hilat Kusha | — | — | — | 10.2 | 12.7 | — | — | — | — | 12.4 | 18.1 | — | — | — | — | 22.1 | 26.5 | — |
| Gamayer | 26.9 | — | — | 20.0 | 21.7 | — | 13.5 | — | — | 13.5 | 16.7 | — | 26.6 | — | — | 25.4 | 26.4 | — |
| Zagalona 1 | 19.9 | — | — | 29.8 | 24.7 | 24.7 | 11.3 | — | — | 12.2 | 13.9 | — | 26.7 | — | — | 17.9 | 20.2 | — |
| Zagalona 2 | 10.8 | — | — | 28.2 | 20.4 | — | 12.7 | — | — | — | 18.9 | — | 32.1 | — | — | 27.2 | 21.0 | — |
| El Meweleh | 28.5 | — | — | 33.5 | 26.3 | — | 19.2 | — | — | 14.6 | 14.5 | — | 25.5 | — | — | 17.1 | 21.1 | — |
| Angola | 11.1 | 5.5 | 9.8 | 18.3 | 12.9 | 16.7 | 11.3 | 20.6 | 12.5 | 13.9 | 13.4 | 12.6 | 8.6 | 20.5 | 13.8 | 12.9 | 10.7 | 21.4 |
| El Markhiat | — | — | 25.8 | — | 27.8 | 26.6 | — | — | 26.0 | — | 27.3 | 24.3 | — | — | 30.4 | — | 32.5 | 26.6 |
| Souk Libya | — | — | — | 17.2 | — | 16.4 | — | — | — | 15.4 | — | 12.6 | — | — | — | 20.7 | — | 23.4 |
| Soba | — | — | — | 21.6 | 19.7 | 18.1 | — | — | — | 27.6 | 16.1 | 21.6 | — | — | — | 19.6 | 29.0 | 24.0 |

*Source:* Sudan, Council of Churches, Inter-Aid, Lower Saxony Team, and Goal, *Monthly Reports* (February-July 1990).

children are at greatest risk for severe infection, as shown by high rates of spontaneous abortion, low birth weight, and malnutrition.[6]

Diarrheal diseases are transmitted from person to person via soiled hands and by food and water contaminated by human waste. They are endemic in areas where sanitation and hygienic habits are poor. In general, the highest rates of diarrhea occur during the hot and rainy seasons.

Acute respiratory infections spread through the air, principally in places with a high population density, crowded living conditions, and abrupt seasonal changes. Crowded households are particularly vulnerable to infection. Among the displaced, density per room is high, and most of the family cooking is done inside the room. Thus, infants and young children are exposed early to diseases brought into the home by parents and older siblings. The impact of acute respiratory infection is intensified by malnutrition. For example, in the Philippines, mortality among children hospitalized with acute respiratory infections was far higher for malnourished children than for children of normal nutritional status.[7] Vitamin A deficiency, long recognized as the leading cause of childhood blindness, may also be an important risk factor for respiratory infections.

## Health Delivery Systems for the Displaced

Curative, preventive, and supplementary feeding programs as well as maternal and child health care are provided by foreign relief agencies, the Islamic African Relief Agency (IARA), and the Sudanese Red Crescent (SRC). Among the twenty-seven settlements in Khartoum, twelve have health clinics, and ten have feeding centers. Health personnel for the settlement populations are hired by the relief agencies: the typical clinic is staffed by a medical assistant, a nurse, and a laboratory assistant. All health personnel are certified by the Ministry of Health, and routine cases are handled by settlement health centers. These health services are not restricted to settlement residents but are shared by the population of nearby areas. As a result of heavy patient loads and limited funds, most settlement health centers suffer from shortages of medicine and supplies.

Cases that cannot be handled by settlement health centers are referred to nearby hospitals. What kind of burden, then, do the displaced put on hospitals? Despite popular belief, there is no evidence that the displaced increase hospital burdens: most hospital facilities are located far from the settlements, thus making transportation unaffordable. In addition, the language barrier, particularly for the southern displaced population, limits access to health services.

The displaced settlements are characterized by the absence of sanitation and public health services. There is no garbage collection, food inspection, or insect spraying. Some of the camps (for example, Kusha, which translates as "dumping area") have been built on top of the Khartoum North garbage dump. Other settlements are located near sewage disposal areas (such as Hilat Shouk in Khartoum before the population was moved to Jebel Awlia) or areas traditionally used for drainage (such as Marzoog in Omdurman).

Traditionally, sanitation and public health services are the responsibility of district councils. Council resources, however, have been reduced by city expansion and sharp cuts in government spending on social services, resulting in the reduction of available personnel and equipment. Furthermore, the displaced settlements are officially considered illegal squatter areas. By offering essential services to these areas, authorities believe they will bestow a measure of legitimacy and recognition that will eventually attract more squatters. The authorities fail to recognize that by deliberately neglecting sanitation they not only endanger the health of the displaced but also the health of the settled population in adjacent areas.

In an effort to provide sanitation services, some relief agencies adopted food-for-work programs; but when the food supply ran out, work completely stopped. Other NGOs attempted to hire trucks for garbage collection, but lack of funds made that effort impossible. Although agencies tried to involve the community in sanitation campaigns, the transient nature of the population and its continuous movement from one settlement to another prohibited any sense of community. The displaced population lives with the daily threat of eviction and has no incentive to invest money and effort into keeping a community clean.

Water shortage has also contributed to the general health of the displaced population. Water is brought into the settlements by donkey carts and sold at high prices, thus limiting the quantity that people can afford to buy. Water quality and quantity have major effects on health. First, poor-quality water may carry pathogens that infect the drinker and cause microbiological diseases such as cholera and typhoid. Second, clean water improves hygiene when used for washing and cooking, thus reducing the incidence of diarrheal, skin, eye, and ectoparasitic diseases (such as louse-borne typhus).[8] Finally, families without running water in the house must draw water and store it. This increases the risk of pollution because containers may be contaminated and water may stagnate. When washing and cooking depend on stored water, use is necessarily limited and the risk of infection rises.

## Child Health in Displaced Settlements

One indicator of child health is the level of malnutrition among young children. Malnutrition is a result not only of deficiency in food intake, but also of a child's exposure to repeated infections that affect the body's use of nutrients. It increases susceptibility to infection and is a strong predictor of a child's chance of survival. Malnutrition is measured by an individual's deviation from a standard population's weight-for-age (W/A), height-for-age (H/A), or weight-for-height (W/H).[9]

Nutrition surveys conducted by the nutrition unit of the Sudan Council of Churches (SCC) in the council's settlement camps in greater Khartoum showed the prevalence of malnutrition among children under age five. Table 5.2 indicates that malnutrition levels declined between September 1989 and March 1990, perhaps due to the impact of seasonal factors on the prevalence of diarrheal diseases

Table 5.2. Percentage of Displaced Children with Less Than 80 Percent Weight-for-Height, September 1989 and March 1990

| Settlement | September 1989 | March 1990 |
|---|---|---|
| Hilat Shouk | 14.4 | 8.1 |
| Hilat Kusha | 12.1 | 5.2 |
| Kalakla | 12.3 | 4.4 |
| Zagalona 1 | 10.9 | 4.0 |
| Muwelih | 7.7 | 2.7 |
| Gamayer | 7.3 | 2.4 |
| Zagalona 2 | 7.5 | 1.6 |

*Source:* Sudan Council of Churches, *Report on Nutrition Surveys Conducted in Eight Settlements for the Displaced around Khartoum* (March 1990).

(which are likely to increase during or after the rainy season), to improved employment opportunities for the displaced, or to a drop in the flow of new arrivals. The table also shows that the settlements of Shouk, Kusha, Kalakla, and Zagalona 1 have the highest rates of child malnutrition: they are among the poorest settlements and were built in the most unsanitary locations (particularly Kusha in Khartoum North).

Malnutrition is most prevalent among children younger than two years, a pattern partly attributed to poor weaning practices. Diarrheal diseases associated with weaning food, lack of food, and poor sanitation conditions may all be contributing factors. Malnutrition is also associated with the father's presence or absence and the mother's employment status. Absence of the father means a sharp reduction in a family's earning capacity, which may push the mother into the labor force. Studies have shown that working mothers are frequently unable to care for their children properly and that young children are left under the care of older siblings or neighbors, which may adversely affect child health.

The Nutrition Department of the Ministry of Health conducted a six-round survey of the twenty-seven displaced settlements in greater Khartoum during July 1990 and July 1991. The survey revealed the poor nutritional status of settlement children, confirming that the level of moderately and severely undernourished children (classified as less than 80 percent of standard weight-for-height) is unacceptably high and a cause for concern. The report also showed a deterioration in the nutritional status of children living in fourteen of the settlements.[10]

Several settlement health centers have provided information about the nutritional status of young children. Table 5.3 reflects the large variations in the rate of malnutrition among children in different settlements as well as differences in nutritional status during different months in the same settlement. Intersettlement comparisons reflect differences in the socioeconomic conditions of settlement populations. For example, the settlements run by SCC (the last five camps shown on the table) are the poorest settlements in the Khartoum area. Intrasettlement comparisons by month reflect the impact of seasons on nutritional status, particularly in settlements with relatively poor sanitation and hygienic conditions.

There are supplementary feeding centers in ten of the twenty-seven

Table 5.3. Percentage of Displaced Children with Less Than 80 Percent Weight-for-Height among Children Who Visited Health Centers in Selected Settlements in Khartoum, February-August 1990

| | Month | | | | | |
|---|---|---|---|---|---|---|
| Settlement | Feb. | Apr. | May | June | July | Aug. |
| Meiyo 1 | — | — | 19.3* | 7.9 | 12.1 | — |
| Meiyo 2 | — | — | 19.0* | 11.8 | 17.6 | 17.9 |
| Soba | — | — | 12.8 | 14.6 | 23.7 | — |
| Markhiat 19 | — | 7.2 | — | 7.6 | 4.6 | — |
| Markhiat 21 | — | 2.8 | 3.9 | 5.1 | 8.9 | — |
| Markhiat 29 | 2.3 | 2.5 | 5.9 | 4.9 | 5.7 | — |
| Khoder | — | — | — | 16.6 | 28.6 | 37.8 |
| Souk Libya | — | — | 22.9 | — | 25.0 | 31.3 |
| Hilat Kusha | 37.5 | — | — | 93.3 | — | — |
| Zagalona | 22.7 | — | — | 62.5 | — | — |
| Gamayer | 50.0 | — | — | 62.5 | — | — |
| Kalakla | 43.3 | — | — | 60.5 | — | — |
| Hilat Shouk | 48.2 | — | — | 76.7 | — | — |

*Source:* Goal, Inter-Aid, and Sudan Council of Churches, *Monthly Reports* (Khartoum, 1990).
*Indicates weight-for-height less than 85 percent.

displaced settlements in greater Khartoum, but only a tiny percentage of malnourished children are enrolled in feeding programs, perhaps because much of the displaced population is unaware the programs exist. Most of the supplementary food programs are clinic based; therefore, people searching for work, particularly women who have to carry children to a feeding center every day, may not have time to visit the programs. In addition, recent food shortages have terminated some supplementary feeding programs.

Data from various settlements show that nearly one-third of the children enrolled in supplementary feeding programs lose weight, usually because supplementary food is substituted for regular home food, other family members eat the child's food, or the child has been exposed to infection that prevents his or her body from metabolizing food at a normal rate. Studies also show that supplementary feeding programs may not be effective in improving childhood nutritional status for a variety of reasons, including their failure to change home environments or to consider the dynamics of food allocation at home.[11]

I cannot objectively assess the immunization programs in settlement camps because the data on immunization against prevalent childhood diseases (tetanus, measles, polio, tuberculosis, diphtheria, and whooping cough) do not consider children under the age of five. Nevertheless, skepticism about health benefits, costs in family time and money, and a high turnover rate in settlement population contribute to reducing immunization coverage. In addition, logistical problems such as gasoline shortages limit the mobility and efficiency of immunization teams.

## Conclusion

Sudan's displaced population is routinely exposed to health risks such as malaria, respiratory-tract infections, diarrheal diseases, eye and skin infections, vitamin A deficiency, and tuberculosis. All are caused by poverty, poor sanitation, and an unhealthy environment. Living conditions are the major contributor to these health problems: most displaced people live in squatter shanties made of sacks, tin, tents, or mud. (Only people who have lived in Khartoum for a long time can afford mud houses.) Crowded living quarters and a dense population have facilitated the spread of communicable diseases, particularly among children.

Relief agencies provide a majority of the curative health facilities in displaced settlements, yet most facilities lack laboratory services and essential medications, particularly antibiotics and antimalarial drugs for children. Even if a health center has access to a laboratory or medications, patients must pay for them, a situation that limits the population's access to health services.

Sanitation services do not exist in displaced settlements because of institutional and funding problems. The absence of basic public health services creates a hazard for both the displaced population and adjacent communities.

To combat the health problems of the displaced, authorities should move squatter settlements away from dumps and drainage areas to locations that supply basic amenities, particularly clean water. Before any relocation, however, the settlement population should be consulted. New locations should be close enough to the city to give the people access to jobs and schools.

It is also important to integrate the role of voluntary relief organizations with a general service-provision policy for the displaced. Without relief organizations to provide valuable services, particularly those related to health, the displaced population would otherwise go without. Nevertheless, the efficiency of those services will be improved by more cooperation and less skepticism from local and central government authorities.

Chapter 6

# The Displaced, Food Production, and Food Aid

*Hatim A. Mahran*

During 1984–85 Sudan experienced a severe drought that led enormous numbers of rural people, particularly from eastern and western Sudan, to migrate to urban centers. The effects of that season's drought were not limited to crop failure but extended to serious livestock losses; they were further aggravated by the late response of the central government, which for political reasons was unwilling to declare a state of emergency to deal with the crisis. Nonetheless, in response to "Sudan Call," the international community eventually provided food aid.

This chapter attempts to clarify the drought's impact on the displaced, food production, food aid, and national security. In the process I contend that food aid (also called relief) has had adverse effects not only on food production and consumption, but also on the entire social organization of food-aid recipients. I begin with a discussion of the size of the problem, then analyze the effects of the drought on food production, and move to Sudan's position as a recipient of food aid relative to other food-recipient countries. Finally, I mention several aspects of the political economy of food aid and offer some concluding remarks.

## The Size of the Problem

The 1983 outbreak of civil war in southern Sudan, coupled with the 1984–85 drought, contributed to massive displacement among affected people in the south and west. According to available statistics, the total number of the displaced reached approximately 6.8 million in 1988. Assuming an annual rate of population growth of 2.5 percent (based on a total population of 20.6 million in 1983), the total population in 1988 can be estimated at 23.9 million. Therefore, in 1988 the displaced population in Sudan constituted 29.1 percent of the total population, a very high proportion by all standards. Table 6.1 shows the total number of displaced by reason of displacement and region of destination. The drought displaced amount to 2.68 million people, while the security displaced (because of war in the south and the west) amount to 4.1 million. In other words, the drought displaced constitute 39.5 percent of the total displaced population, and the security displaced represent 60.5 percent. As a proportion of the total 1988 population, the drought displaced represent 11.2 percent, while the security displaced represent 17.6 percent.

Concerning the distribution of the displaced by region of destination, the data in table 6.1 reveal that greater Khartoum bears the brunt of the problem: it received 26.6 percent of the total number of displaced in 1988. Furthermore, the 1.8 million displaced people who live in greater Khartoum have significantly crowded the area; for every one hundred original inhabitants, there are now more than eighty-five displaced persons. The 1988 figures suggest that the dis-

Table 6.1. Number of Displaced People, by Reason of Displacement and Region of Destination, 1988 (in millions)

| | Reason | | |
|---|---|---|---|
| Region | Security | Drought | Total |
| Northern | 0.08 | 0.08 | 0.16 |
| Khartoum | 1.80 | — | 1.80 |
| Central | 0.32 | 0.20 | 0.52 |
| Eastern | — | 0.60 | 0.60 |
| Darfur | 0.06 | 0.80 | 0.86 |
| Kordofan | 0.07 | 1.00 | 1.07 |
| Bahr Elghazal | 0.41 | — | 0.41 |
| Equatoria | 0.80 | — | 0.80 |
| Upper Nile | 0.56 | — | 0.56 |
| Total | 4.10 | 2.68 | 6.78 |

*Source:* Commissions for Displaced and Relief and Rehabilitation (Khartoum).

placed in Khartoum constitute nearly 47 percent of the city's population.

Sudan is an agrarian economy; agriculture contributes about 40 percent of GDP and generates more than 90 percent of the country's foreign exchange earnings. More important, the agrarian sector produces food crops to meet both rural and urban demands. Therefore, displacement poses a serious threat not only to rural food security but also to national food security. Faced with an increasing number of displaced people, Sudan may eventually be forced to rely on food aid to mitigate the crisis, which in turn may lead to dependency on imported food and thus have implications for national security.

It is also important to note that the rural displaced face an unfamiliar social organization in recipient regions, particularly in urban areas. This situation may create social conflicts that will eventually pose serious threats to public order. Furthermore, in greater Khartoum, where the displaced represent 47 percent of the region's population, the spread of displaced settlements in the area, coupled with meager government resources, has led to an enormous deterioration in social services. Thus, the displacement problem cannot be solved simply by providing food and shelter; it must also address social services and public order in recipient regions and national security in the country as a whole.

## Production of Food Crops

Sudan's principal food crops are sorghum, millet, and wheat. Millet is grown in rain-fed areas of Darfur and Kordofan, and sorghum is grown both in rain-fed areas (such as Gedarif) and irrigated areas (such as the Gezira scheme). Wheat is grown in irrigated areas, particularly in the north and the Gezira scheme. Thus, poor rainy seasons have a significant impact on sorghum and millet production. Furthermore, because the level of the Nile and its two tributaries determines the amount of water available for irrigation (which in turn is determined by the rainy season) and because wheat competes with export-oriented cotton for irrigation water, a poor rainy season also has significant impact on the wheat crop.

Table 6.2 shows the area and output of Sudan's three main food crops from 1981–82 to 1987–88, a period that illustrates crop trends before, during, and after the 1984–85 drought. The table suggests

Table 6.2. Area and Output of Main Food Crops, 1981-82 to 1987-88*

| Crop | 1981-82 | 1982-83 | 1983-84 | 1984-85 | 1985-86 | 1986-87 | 1987-88 |
|---|---|---|---|---|---|---|---|
| *Sorghum* | | | | | | | |
| Output | 3,345 | 1,964 | 1,828 | 1,097 | 3,542 | 3,277 | 1,379 |
| Area | 8,888 | 8,318 | 8,575 | 7,668 | 12,360 | 11,340 | 8,038 |
| *Millet* | | | | | | | |
| Output | 573 | 333 | 314 | 158 | 428 | 285 | 153 |
| Area | 2,513 | 2,614 | 2,904 | 3,001 | 3,944 | 3,529 | 2,495 |
| *Wheat* | | | | | | | |
| Output | 163 | 141 | 169 | 79 | 199 | 157 | 181 |
| Area | 340 | 224 | 335 | 110 | 346 | 271 | 328 |

*Source:* Bank of Sudan, *Annual Report* (Khartoum, 1988).
*Output in thousands of metric tons and area in thousands of acres.

that crop production has oscillated over the years. For example, during 1984–85, crop output—particularly of rain-fed millet—reached its lowest level in comparison with other years. Overall, that year's sorghum, millet, and wheat crops decreased by 40 percent, 49.7 percent, and 53.3 percent respectively when compared with 1983–84 levels. This drastic fall in output may have been caused by a decrease in cultivated land, a fall in labor productivity, or both; and each factor can be attributed to severe drought conditions. No data are available on labor productivity or employment. Nevertheless, because the drought resulted in massive displacement of rural people, particularly from western Sudan, farmers who remained on the land were probably not able to compensate for the loss in labor supply. This contention is supported by two considerations. First, the drought and the consequent food shortage may have affected the health of those who remained on the farm; and second, food-aid deliveries resulted in further loss of work hours. Farmers, who under normal circumstances spend most of their time on the farm, found themselves spending long hours in relief lines for food rations.

The data in table 6.2 can also be used to compute yield per acre of the three main food crops. Overall, sorghum's yield per acre decreased by 32.9 percent, and the total area under sorghum cultivation decreased by 10.6 percent. During the drought of 1984–85, the fall in yield per acre can be attributed mainly to a decrease in output. The effect of the drought was more pronounced on millet: despite a 3.3 percent increase in area under cultivation, crop output fell by 49.7 percent, resulting in a 51.3 percent decline yield per acre compared with 1983–84. Wheat's area under cultivation decreased by 67 percent during 1984–85 when compared with the previous year, probably because of the poor rainy season in Ethiopia, which affected the level of the Nile and the amount of water available for irrigation. In spite of wheat's fall in output, yield per acre has improved 41.9 percent from 1983–84.

During the successful rainy season of 1985–86, overall crop output and area improved significantly. Sorghum output, area, and yield per acre increased by 222.9 percent, 61.2 percent, and 100.4 percent respectively; millet also improved (output, 170.9 percent; area, 31.5 percent, and yield per acre, 106.3 percent). Wheat's yield per acre, however, decreased by 19.5 percent.

The drought did not limit its effects to food crops; it also caused significant loss of cattle, sheep, goats, and camels. Table 6.3 reports livestock market prices for 1980–84. Using annual prices of cattle, sheep, goats, and camels (adjusted for each year's consumer price index), I calculated the weighted average annual deflated prices of livestock in each market. During 1980–84, livestock prices showed a downward trend, reaching their minimum level in the drought year 1984 when the weighted average price declined by 21.1 percent from its level in 1983. This downward trend may be explained by significant losses in livestock, which forced owners to sell a large proportion of their remaining livestock at low prices to head off further losses.

Data on livestock prices for the postdrought period are not available. I believe, however, that after the successful rainy season in 1985–86, livestock prices started to rise. This change may have resulted from large-scale food-aid deliveries, which reduced the number of livestock offered for sale and thus gradually raised prices.

### Food Aid: Sudan's Position Relative to Other Countries

It is clear that the drought of 1984–85 had a significant impact on food production, and the country's lack of preparation coupled with drought severity forced the government to ask the international community for food relief. *Food aid* may be defined as the amount of food a country needs to fill the gap between its demand for food and its production and import abilities. Alternatively, it may be defined

Table 6.3. Weighted Average Annual Deflated Prices of Livestock in Selected Markets, 1980-84

| Market | 1980 | 1981 | 1982 | 1983 | 1984 |
|---|---|---|---|---|---|
| Nyala | 40.2 | 35.6 | 29.6 | 31.2 | 21.7 |
| El Fashir | 43.6 | 32.8 | 26.1 | 36.6 | 30.4 |
| El Obeid | 38.0 | 34.1 | 30.6 | 33.0 | 22.9 |
| Kosti | 32.7 | 28.0 | 28.9 | 31.3 | 19.2 |
| Wad Medani | 46.5 | 41.0 | 30.2 | 33.2 | 29.9 |
| Omdurman | 47.2 | 43.1 | 34.4 | 34.2 | 31.0 |

*Source:* Calculated from data obtained in Department of Agricultural Economics, Ministry of Agriculture and Natural Resources, "Agricultural Prices in Sudan: A Historical Review and Analysis, 1970-1984" (Khartoum, 1985).

as the amount of food needed to alleviate hunger and reach minimal nutritional standards. No matter how it is measured, the latter need is always far wider than the former because nutritional standards in developing countries are very low.

Table 6.4 shows the distribution of cereal food aid throughout the world from 1987 to 1989. During this period, low-income, food-deficit countries received an average of 84.8 percent of the world's total food aid, leaving only 15.2 percent for all other countries. Low nutritional standards in developing economies translate into high food requirements, and supply bottlenecks mean that these requirements cannot be met by domestic production. Furthermore, because developing economies are characterized by low income, they are unable to fill the food gap by imports. In some cases, these factors may be aggravated by natural disasters such as drought, desertification, and floods that destroy food crops.

Table 6.5 shows cereal food-aid deliveries to selected low-income, food-deficit countries from 1987 to 1989. On average, Egypt received the highest proportion of cereal food aid, followed by Bangladesh, Ethiopia, Sudan, and Pakistan. In fact, Egypt and Bangladesh maintained their first- and second-place positions in each of the three years considered. Sudan's position improved from third in 1987 to sixth in 1988 and 1989, due mainly to government efforts to in-

Table 6.4. Cereal Food-Aid Deliveries Worldwide, 1987-89 (in thousands of tons)*

| | 1987 | 1988 | 1989 | Annual Average |
|---|---|---|---|---|
| Low-Income Food-Deficit Countries | 11,287<br>(88.7) | 11,237<br>(85.5) | 8,657.7<br>(79.2) | 10,393.9<br>(84.8) |
| Other Countries | 1,438.8<br>(11.3) | 1,900.5<br>(14.5) | 2,270.9<br>(20.8) | 1,870.1<br>(15.2) |
| World Total | 12,725.8<br>(100) | 13,137.5<br>(100) | 10,928.6<br>(100) | 12,264<br>(100) |

*Source:* Food and Agriculture Organization, "Food Aid Review" (Rome, 1990).
*Figures in parentheses are percentages of the corresponding totals.

Table 6.5. Cereal Food-Aid Deliveries to Selected Low-Income Food Deficit Countries, 1987-89 (in thousands of tons)*

| Country | 1987 | 1988 | 1989 | Average | Rank |
|---|---|---|---|---|---|
| Bangladesh | 1,776.3 | 1,339.6 | 1,299.8 | 1,471.9 | (2) |
| | (15.7) | (11.9) | (15.0) | (14.2) | |
| China | 494.4 | 351.1 | 137.6 | 327.7 | (8) |
| | (4.4) | (3.1) | (1.6) | (3.2) | |
| Egypt | 2,066.4 | 1,414.7 | 1,361.4 | 1,614.2 | (1) |
| | (18.3) | (12.6) | (15.7) | (15.5) | |
| Ethiopia | 409.3 | 1,178.6 | 368.4 | 615.4 | (3) |
| | (3.6) | (10.1) | (5.1) | (6.4) | |
| Morocco | 505.8 | 304.7 | 278.3 | 362.9 | (7) |
| | (4.5) | (2.7) | (3.2) | (3.5) | |
| Mozambique | 401.4 | 589.3 | 488.4 | 493.0 | (6) |
| | (3.6) | (5.2) | (5.6) | (4.7) | |
| Pakistan | 472.6 | 627.7 | 450.2 | 516.8 | (5) |
| | (4.2) | (5.6) | (5.2) | (5.0) | |
| Sri Lanka | 422.9 | 262.0 | 275.1 | 320.0 | (9) |
| | (3.7) | (2.3) | (3.2) | (3.1) | |
| Sudan | 705.9 | 549.9 | 337.8 | 531.2 | (4) |
| | (6.3) | (4.9) | (3.9) | (5.1) | |

*Source:* Food and Agriculture Organization, "Food Aid Review" (Rome, 1990).
*Figures in parentheses are percentages of cereal food aid received by each country relative to cereal food donated to all low-income countries.

crease food-crop area and output after the successful rainy season of 1985–86.

Table 6.4 shows that food-aid deliveries decreased from 1987 to 1989, and donor indications suggest that food aid for developing countries will continue to decline. Thus, a number of low-income, food-deficit countries may face increased difficulties in meeting cereal consumption requirements. Donors continue to target the poorest and most vulnerable people in low-income, food-deficit countries. Therefore, if food availability is reduced, there will also be a reduction in aid for development and a corresponding increase in aid for emergency relief, refugees, and displaced people.[1] I believe that Sudan will continue to be a major recipient of food aid, at least for the displaced, unless some effort is made to increase domestic production of food crops.

## The Political Economy of Food Aid

Sudan has received a considerable amount of food aid as a result of famine and civil war coupled with production bottlenecks and the inability of the national economy to finance adequate food imports. Because of the ongoing civil war, the country will likely continue to be a major recipient of food aid in the future. This situation has been exacerbated by the poor rainy season and consequent drought of 1989–90, which has already forced large numbers of people, particularly westerners, to move to urban centers.

Table 6.6 shows cereal food-aid deliveries to Sudan as a proportion of the cereal food supply in 1986–87 and 1987–88. Although in 1986–87 cereal food aid represented 16 percent of the cereal food supply, that ratio increased in 1987–88 to 24.3 percent. In 1987–88 both cereal food aid and cereal food supply decreased from their levels in 1986–87 (by 22.1 percent and 48.9 percent respectively). Thus, the 1987–88 rise in cereal food aid as compared with the cereal food supply was due mainly to the fact that the decrease in local supply was greater than the decrease in aid, implying a growing dependency on food aid.

Food aid is a central if controversial component of development assistance. Despite its humanitarian intentions, particularly during famine and natural disasters, it continues to draw a wide range of

Table 6.6. Cereal Food Aid, Output, and Supply in Sudan, 1986-87, 1987-88 (in thousands of tons)*

| | 1986-87 | 1987-88 | % Change |
|---|---|---|---|
| Aid | 705.9 | 549.9 | -22.1 |
| | (16.0) | (24.3) | |
| Output | 3,719.0 | 1,713.0 | -53.9 |
| | (84.0) | (75.7) | |
| Total Supply | 4,424.9 | 2,262.9 | -48.9 |
| | (100) | (100) | |

*Sources:* Food and Agriculture Organization, "Food Aid Review" (Rome, 1990). Output calculations based on data from Bank of Sudan, "Annual Report" (Khartoum, 1988). This is the sum of sorghum, millet, and wheat output.

*Figures in parentheses show cereal food aid and output as a percentage of total cereal food supply.

criticism. Some people argue that food aid can make important contributions to employment and economic growth as well as to consumption stability in developing countries. Their argument centers on two important considerations. First, food aid extends resources beyond other forms of development assistance. In answer to this argument, however, one might pose a legitimate question: if food aid extends beyond any other form of assistance, why shouldn't it be donated in the form of money? The answer is complex. During a famine, for example, no one is against food aid; under such circumstances, it is the only way to save lives at risk. In addition, food aid continues to receive substantial political support from farm groups in donor countries who consider it an outlet for the abundant food they produce. Thus, even if money replaced actual food donations, those funds would still be allocated to food purchases from the donor country.

The second argument asserts that food aid checks rising food prices and hence encourages employment and economic growth in food-aid recipient countries. In developing economies, the abundant labor force may be mobilized to produce a wide range of labor-intensive goods, including wage goods such as food. Nevertheless, due to production rigidities and laborers' propensity to spend wages on food (which translates into a high demand for food), food deficits arise, with the inevitable consequence of rising food prices and wages. This situation places a significant constraint on labor mobilization. Some people argue that under such circumstances food supplies are needed to prevent the increase in food prices and wages that might otherwise reduce the demand for labor. Because food aid is the only source through which additional food is supplied, many believe that it plays a critical role in relieving the pressure on food supplies, thus reducing food prices and wages and enhancing employment and growth. In short, food aid may provide an important stimulus for development by supplying the wage goods needed to stimulate labor mobilization and growth.

The second argument rests on the effect of food aid on the price mechanism of local agriculture. Labor mobilization depends on the interaction of two markets: food and labor. As food prices fall, the labor force receives a larger share of the total wage bill, most of which is spend on food. This, in turn, stimulates further employment. But when food prices fall, wages may fall by the same proportion or even less, meaning that real wages remain the same or increase. Schultz (1960), for example, argues that if food aid is sold on the open market, prices tend to fall below what they would otherwise have been, therefore discouraging agricultural production and the overall level of food availability. After Sudan's 1984–85 famine, emergency food aid to the affected people in Kordofan and Darfur regions (where the effects of the drought were most pronounced) resulted in a decrease in cereal food prices that discouraged domestic cereal production.[2]

Unfortunately, when food aid is used to solve short-term problems of food supply, it often diverts the attention of policymakers from agricultural development. Dependency, both of governments and citizens, is the inherent result. Indeed, the impact of emergency food aid to Sudan has affected long-established traditions in Sudanese society. Due to the severity of the drought, the displaced people of Kordofan and Darfur were not only prepared to accept food aid, but were also willing to spend long hours in line waiting for it.[3] The displaced came to believe that the government and food-relief organizations were responsible for providing food indefinitely, whether or not there was a crisis.

No one opposes food aid that is made available for purely humanitarian reasons, but does all food aid meet that requirement? Some people have argued that many donors use food aid to achieve economic or political goals. For example, food is sometimes offered to developing countries to expand sales and secure future markets. Donors achieve this long-term goal by changing the recipient society's consumption pattern, often by feeding children who form the basis of future food markets. It has also been argued that food aid replaces direct military intervention as an effective means of achieving political or economic goals, particularly when military intervention is not feasible or is politically unacceptable.

## Conclusion

This chapter attempts to clarify the impact of drought on the displaced population as well as on food production, food aid, and national security. No matter what causes displacement, the solution cannot be limited to food and shelter; it must also address national security. The ongoing civil war in the south and recent droughts have resulted in the displacement of large numbers of people who pose serious threats to health, education, and security services in recipient areas, particularly greater Khartoum.

The drought of 1984–85 had an enormous impact on cereal production. Although sorghum and wheat production both reached low levels that season, rain-fed millet was particularly hard hit. Low production levels were directly related to the labor loss created by displacement, poor nutritional status among farm families, and work hours lost in relief lines.

The severity of the drought coupled with a lack of preparation forced the government to ask the international community for food aid. Today, because of drought and the ongoing war in the south, Sudan continues to receive a significant amount of aid. Given the country's meager foreign exchange resources and its inability to import food, Sudan's dependency on food aid will only increase. Unfortunately, the motives of many donors are not strictly humanitarian. In many cases, economic and political goals mean that donors use food to promote future markets in recipient economies and thus guarantee dependency.

Chapter 7

# Management of Relief for the Displaced: The Experience of Sudan

*Omer Elmugly*

This chapter assesses the ability of Sudan's administrative structure to handle the country's displacement crisis, a situation that requires prompt response to avoid enormous social and economic costs. Efficient relief management is difficult when the government has no control over relief supply or demand in a situation in which millions of lives are at stake. In addition, management efficiency is important whenever individuals and institutions are combining efforts to attain a single goal.

I make two distinctions in my discussion of relief management. The first is the distinction between managerial functions (planning, organization, coordination, communication, control) and operational functions (securing relief supplies, storage, transport, distribution). Although these two categories overlap, I make a distinction between who does what. Managerial functions have significant input from top executives and policymakers, whereas operational functions are directly handled by executives and staff. In this chapter I emphasize managerial functions.

My second distinction concerns the difference between management by process and management by results. *Management by process* gives priority to rules and regulations, sometimes irrespective of the final outcome. This style prevails in government administration, creating a passive attitude among civil servants and a "follow the rules no matter what" mentality. Such a style is unsuitable for relief management, which requires a dynamic, flexible structure to cope with a volatile and rapidly changing task environment. I call this style *management by results*: attention is focused on actual results before taking necessary corrective measures. My distinction between styles does not imply that management by results ignores or undermines rules, regulations, and procedures; rather, it perceives them as a way to achieve stated goals instead of an end in themselves. Management by results gives goals and direction to relief management agencies and allows flexibility, sensitivity, and efficiency.

Anyone studying a management situation in the public sector, particularly in a country like Sudan, which has an underdeveloped administrative system, has to consider the following:

- A variety of agencies may be involved in decision making, and coordination problems may have several causes: (1) different perceptions about the objective, (2) professional tribalism, or a reluctance caused by the belief that an effort or decision is one agency's job and not another's, and (3) lack of knowledge or expertise.
- Politicians, who are inevitably involved in decision making, tend to interfere with all aspects of government business in an attempt to promote their image as guardians of the public interest, sometimes with the deliberate intention of serving individual or party interests.
- Inadequate planning mechanisms make it necessary to resort to ad hoc measures, particularly in a crisis.
- The bureaucratic nature of government administration creates red tape and slow decision making.
- There is low morale among civil servants, mainly due to low pay and lack of appreciation. Therefore, government officials often feel indifferent about the actual outcome of a decision, try to avoid responsibility, and may ultimately become susceptible to corruption.
- The government administrative system is centralized both geographically and structurally; most influential powers are based in the national capital, and organizational power is concentrated in the hands of senior executives. Such centralized power generates a lack of confidence among citizens, who do not believe their regional governments can offer help.

## Management of Relief

The severe drought of 1984–85, the resulting famine, and the 1983 outbreak of war in the south led many people to flee their homelands in search of food and security. The initial government response to this displacement was passive. The administration believed that acknowledgment of famine would be politically embarrassing and could undermine government efforts to attract foreign investors to finance Sudan's overpublicized "breadbasket policy." For a time the government maintained its passivity despite warnings from voluntary organizations such as the Sudanese Red Crescent and the Islamic African Relief Agency, who understood the implications of the 1983 crop failure. Those organizations published data reflecting the prices of sorghum, livestock, and other foodstuffs and studied the population migration from hard-hit Kordofan and Darfur.

In response to international pressure, the government was eventually forced to face the enormity of the disaster and disclosed the extent of the crisis in July 1984. At first it limited its intervention: it declared Darfur a disaster area and set up a relief committee to handle the situation there. Before long, however, the government acknowledged the full extent of the crisis and formed the Military Commission for the Management of Relief (Ministerial Decree 52, 1 August 1984). This action was followed on 15 November 1984 by the formation of the Supreme Commission for Relief to manage relief supplies to El Muwelih and Abu Zeid, makeshift camps on the outskirts of Omdurman with a heavy concentration of displaced people from the west. On 24 December 1984 a presidential decree established the Supreme Commission for the Combat of Disasters, Drought, and Desertification; and the process culminated with the creation of the Relief and Rehabilitation Commission (RRC) in 1986 and the Commission of the Displaced (COD) in 1988.

The ad hoc nature of these organizational arrangements is clearly reflected by their frequent and unfounded change in form and substance as well as their lack of articulate policy and vision. An official of the COD highlighted some early relief management problems:

- Inadequate planning due to irregular, unreliable information flow

- Inadequate infrastructure, particularly in transport arrangements
- Lack of national expertise
- Security problems, especially in the south and in western Darfur
- Loose administrative structures
- Lack of an early warning system

To this list we can add the difficulties created by the institutional relief structure, which were manifest in frequent political and policy changes, organizational discontinuity when government ministries were dissolved and created, the tendency of politicians without vision to interfere in relief operations, and the archaic nature of government procedures and rules.

The interagency nature of relief management has been well established in Sudan. Although the two main agencies are the RRC and the COD, other departments and organizations also play important roles. In some cases, an agency primarily coordinates the contributions of others, a point emphasized often in conferences on relief. For example, the 1986 RRC Act states that the agency's creation increases the need for coordination at the policy formulation level, which means that its board of directors must be composed of representatives from all relevant government agencies to ensure close coordination at high levels. Nevertheless, as I discuss later, the issue of coordination or the lack of it has proved to be an enormous obstruction to the smooth, efficient management of relief.

## The Relief and Rehabilitation Commission

The 1986 act that created the RRC states: "Given the distinct nature of relief and rehabilitation projects for whose management the traditional government procedures and resources are deemed inadequate, the commission will make use of the existing technical facilities available to the ministries as well as foreign aid, to implement on project basis necessary plans and programs which could lead to combating the adverse consequences of natural disasters and resettle the affected people."

For the most part the RRC is treated as an ordinary government department, except for certain distinctions mentioned in its establishing act. That act calls for the formation of a board of directors representing all concerned agencies. They are selected by the prime minister to formulate RRC policy, follow up on policy decisions, and oversee implementation. Originally the commissioner, RRC's chief executive officer, was appointed to state minister status by the prime minister and reported directly to him. The commissioner's status changed, however, when the RRC merged with a government ministry, a problem I will discuss later in this section.

The act also stipulates certain RRC functions:

- Collecting and classifying relevant information and indicators that warn about impending disaster and sending necessary signals to concerned agencies
- Raising and coordinating local and international relief aid
- Organizing and coordinating relief operations in disaster areas
- Conducting research to help avoid or alleviate disaster
- Cooperating with relevant agencies to protect and maintain natural resources and the environment
- Rehabilitating disaster-affected areas
- Promoting national awareness about the importance of protecting natural resources
- Conducting scientific conferences and seminars in RRC areas of activity
- Seeking the support of relevant agencies when implementing stated policies
- Supervising the activities of international organizations and NGOs involved in relief and rehabilitation as well as assessing their performance and directing their programs to meet the real needs of the country

Interviews with RRC officials often indicate that this list of functions is too ambitious, given the commission's physical, financial, and human resources and the organizational constraints to which it is subject.

The organizational history of the RRC tells an all-too-familiar story: frequent ad hoc organizational changes leading ultimately to organizational discontinuity, changes in leadership, changes in management philosophy, and the generation of fluidity and uncertainty. For example, when the RRC was first set up in 1986, it was headed by a commissioner with state minister status. RRC staff and clients perceived the commissioner's status as a structural benefit that could facilitate cooperation with the central government. When the commission became part of the new Ministry for Relief, Rehabilitation, and the Displaced, however, the commissioner reported to the minister in charge rather than the prime minister, creating widespread resentment among RRC staff members.

Unstructured and uninformed interference in commission operations was commonplace among senior politicians during the RRC's reorganizational period, particularly during the severe floods that struck the country in 1988. As a result, confusion ensued over relief management. Because it was not clear who was responsible for what, politicking and corruption began to invade the commission—so much so that one donor country refused to release its donated funds. The government that took office in 1989 eventually dissolved the Ministry for Relief, Rehabilitation, and the Displaced and assigned the RRC to the minister of commerce—not the ministry.

RRC's interface with other government agencies has not been entirely successful, as shown by yet-to-be-resolved disputes between the RRC and the ministries of finance and agriculture. Officials in the planning department at the Ministry of Finance see themselves as custodians of all foreign aid, while officials of the RRC believe that relief aid should be channeled through the commission. The Ministry of Agriculture dispute focuses on responsibility for combating desertification, a program viewed by the RRC as an integral part of rehabilitation. The RRC wants a group of well-equipped specialists to handle this operation, but the Ministry of Agriculture is not ready to relinquish its power in the matter, forcing the commission to settle for a coordination and follow-up role in desertification projects. The RRC has also clashed with the COD over supplying relief materials for distribution among the displaced. Because the agencies have no established mechanism of coordination, any cooperation is ad hoc.

It is clear that horizontal coordination between the RRC and its peer agencies is weak, to say the least. Vertical coordination between central, regional, and local authorities is no better. The commission has established several regional offices; but due to aging communication facilities (or the lack of them) and irregular information flow, the RRC finds it difficult to coordinate vertically. Thus, the regional offices and regional governments are left to themselves to see that relief flows to affected people.

The NGOs have a special office at RRC headquarters, supposedly to facilitate cooperation with the commission. Nevertheless, the RRC's follow-up of NGO activities remains inefficient because of the commission's poor communication facilities, which cannot match the NGOs' sophisticated equipment and organization.

The RRC's stated responsibilities, particularly those related to rehabilitation, imply the need for planning. After the commission's policy shift from relief to rehabilitation (in other words, working to make the displaced productive members of the community), the rehabilitation department proposed several projects based on studies conducted by RRC staff and submitted these proposals to potential donors. Despite RRC efforts, donor cooperation does not seem to be forthcoming; instead, donors seem to be emphasizing relief for political reasons.

Recognizing the importance of predicting disasters, the RRC set up an early-warning system that operates in conjunction with relevant government agencies and issues a regular monthly bulletin. In addition, a data collection unit has been activated, and a computer system is being installed to help process data into meaningful planning information. A more recent development is the RRC's adoption of the "Food for Work" scheme sponsored by the World Food Program. This scheme proposes to make disaster-affected people more self-reliant by offering them a means of production rather than temporary relief. Many displaced people have welcomed the scheme because it gives them the chance to rehabilitate their land.

Despite some well-intentioned efforts, however, the RRC continues to have many shortcomings:

- RRC projects are being implemented by other agencies, implying a gap between policy formulation and implementation, which makes it organizationally difficult for the commission to oversee implementation.
- The RRC seems to ignore the importance of eliciting effective participation from the displaced to ensure their enthusiastic involvement in planned projects, although the need for this approach has often been stressed. Such popular participation could begin during research studies and continue through final project assessment.

· Although the RRC's planned projects are intended to combat dependency on donations, most of the funds for these projects are still expected to come from abroad. The commission needs to raise as much money as possible from local sources and try to enlist the aid of Sudanese entrepreneurs.

The RRC's lack of efficient communication and follow-up is most evident in its attempt to exert control over relief. A shortage of technical resources and internal problems within the organization make it nearly impossible for the RRC to control relief supplies effectively and efficiently. Unfortunately, commission inefficiency has allowed self-centered officials and popular leaders to divert relief supplies for their own personal benefit. As one RRC official told me, corruption has spread across the sociopolitical spectrum, from ministers to manual workers. Although technical problems at the commission have encouraged corruption, the RRC also lacks the authority it needs to put an end to violations and is weakened by the ad hoc intervention of politicians, who tend to overrule the commission and interfere in their own behalf. This situation was made very clear during the 1988 floods when several politicians formed ad hoc committees to manage the distribution of relief, thus completely bypassing the RRC.

## Commission of the Displaced

By 1986 the estimated number of displaced Sudanese had grown to 5.5 million, most of them scattered throughout the relatively secure northern regions of the country, particularly in central Sudan and greater Khartoum. Recognizing the ever-increasing social, economic, and political problems of displacement, the government set up the National Council for the Displaced in January 1988, an organization composed of thirty-four representatives from relevant government agencies. In late 1988 the council was converted to the Commission of the Displaced, which aims to manage relief supplies for the displaced and seek ways to accomplish resettlement.

The ministerial decree establishing the commission stated that the commissioner, who is the chief executive of the organization, should report to the minister of relief, refugees, and the displaced. When that ministry was dissolved, the COD was assigned to the Ministry of Social Welfare. Thus, the agency has a lower organizational status than the RRC, whose commissioner (at least on paper) is supposed to report to the prime minister. Many officials at the COD are dissatisfied with the commission's position in the hierarchy, believing they would maintain more autonomy if the commissioner were supervised by the prime minister.

The establishment decree also indicates that vacant jobs at the commission will be filled from other government departments or through transfer of redundant staff, a practice also followed at the RRC. Unfortunately, this staffing procedure means that the COD can be used as a dumping ground for inefficient employees who still remain loyal to their old departments. Even worse, these employees may prefer to cling to established habits, thus threatening harmony and understanding within the COD.

The commission has regional offices throughout Sudan except in the south and the east. According to one COD official, those two regions are excluded because they send out displaced people rather than receive them. Such a perspective shows a lack of foresight; by staying out of the south and the east, the COD has no chance to contain the problem at its source. Sometimes the regional setup means that multiple groups handle a single issue. For example, the COD regional office in Khartoum reports directly to the governor of Khartoum, not COD headquarters, primarily because the Khartoum branch was established before the main office. This means that the governor has a great deal of policy influence in a region with a heavy concentration of displaced people. Indeed, one newspaper reported that the governor of Khartoum took responsibility for discussing government plans for the displaced with the director of Oxfam.[1]

The director of administrative affairs at the COD has commented that the central office does not promote effective cooperation with the RRC, a view also held by RRC officials. Many of these coordination problems stem from a belief that the COD's main function, unlike the RRC's, is to resettle the displaced. Most relief supplies, however, are channeled through the RRC for COD distribution. In addition, with the shift in emphasis from relief to rehabilitation, the two agencies have a chance to work together on joint rehabilitation-resettlement projects. In a policy statement, the commissioner of the COD emphasized a long-term plan to launch rehabilitation and resettlement programs in the homelands, a project that coincides with RRC policies and thus necessitates closer cooperation between the two agencies.

Similar cooperation is required between the COD and more than two hundred NGOs, some of which are involved in distributing relief or implementing resettlement projects. There have been widespread allegations that certain NGOs sell their aid for sociopolitical influence and need closer monitoring and follow-up from the COD. But like the RRC, the COD is handicapped by poor communication facilities and an irregular flow of information, which makes monitoring the NGOs difficult.

A recent COD policy statement describes the commission's short-, medium-, and long-term plans. All of them emphasize the shift from relief to resettlement, an approach that coincides with the RRC's policy approach. This shift is based on a widespread belief among COD staff members that the most appropriate solution for displacement is resettlement in homelands, which can be accomplished by providing security and productive work schemes. In 1989 the COD research and planning department submitted several planning proposals to the United Nations Development Program and the Ministry of Finance. Two funded agricultural projects in the Upper Nile region, one in Wad Dakona and the other in Abu Khadra, have effectively slowed the flow of people from the area. Similar projects in Abu Ajoora (in southern Darfur), Malakal, and western Equatoria have also proven successful. Donor countries have agreed to several other proposals, most important the provision of storage facilities at Babanousa to supply radio communication and transport (at an estimated cost of more than six million dollars) and the construction of an airport. The project, which will be financed by Italy, the Netherlands, the United States, and the United Nations Development Program, aims to keep sufficient relief supplies near the southern regional border to halt the exodus of people fleeing war and drought. Such a project could have solved problems for both the government and the displaced if it had been implemented earlier.

In one area the COD seems to be moving in the right direction: the commission is emphasizing the need to involve the displaced in planning and implementing resettlement projects. This point has been reiterated in many COD policy documents as well as during the 1990 National Conference on Displacement. Currently the COD in

Khartoum sponsors regular weekly meetings among sultans, popular leaders of the displaced, and the commissioner. They discuss ways to overcome logistical problems in camps and plan for repatriation. This practice needs to extend to other regions, whether through the COD's regional offices or regional governments, because many displaced people are hesitant about returning home.

One major obstruction to the COD's planning efforts is the irregular flow of information, particularly the absence of accurate statistics about the number of displaced people. The commission also has no early-warning system. According to one senior official, the first time the agency ever planned ahead of disaster occurred when the deputy governor of one southern region visited COD offices a week before an imminent crisis to ask for precautionary arrangements. In addition, the commission, like the RRC, faces institutional problems such as lack of effective coordination, financial red tape at the central office, and the politics of foreign aid.

## Conclusion

In this chapter I have focused on the managerial functions of relief institutions, which if properly delivered can make life easier for the displaced and those managing their affairs. To be fair we must look at relief management in the context of public-sector management. Red tape, lengthy procedures, unstructured and uninformed interference, and ad hoc approaches are common to most government administrative structures. Unfortunately, Sudan's relief management agencies have failed to avoid those pitfalls.

Effective planning for relief and rehabilitation is hindered by a lack of sufficient resources, particularly those needed for collecting and processing data; the division between policy formulation and implementation, which hampers effective follow-up; limited financial resources, which make government institutions vulnerable to donor politicking; and insufficient input from the displaced. The organizational structures of the RRC and the COD have been subject to frequent change, creating instability and discontinuity, and delegated authorities have not been able to accomplish goals. Both vertical and horizontal coordination have suffered from the loose nature of government structures and the tendency of officials to defend their own professional careers and expand their own powers. As a result, relief agencies cannot exert effective control, making it difficult for officials to identify problems in order to correct them.

As a solution for some of those mistakes, I suggest the following:

- Because it is crucial to stress the autonomy of relief and rehabilitation agencies, they should report directly to the prime minister. They should not, however, be transformed into a ministry. (The ministry model has been tried and does not seem promising.) Equally important is the need for competent, high-caliber leaders who can influence the government decision-making process and convince others to cooperate. Any chief executive must have sufficient authority to move freely within the policy framework approved by the government.
- Planning capabilities can be strengthened by increased expertise, an adequate information infrastructure, and a closer union between policy formulation and implementation.
- The RRC and the COD should be merged into one agency in charge of relief, rehabilitation, and resettlement. With sufficient authority and effective leadership, a combined agency will be better able to coordinate with peer agencies and NGOs.
- An effective early-warning system includes expanding the role of regional offices (which must serve all regions). Because regional offices are closer to potential disaster areas, they should be equipped to prevent or contain the situation rather than wait for it to explode. The main office should be equally ready to coordinate central and regional efforts.
- Progress should be thoroughly assessed at regular intervals to correct errors in due time. There must be a balance between the control needed to prevent corruption and the flexibility needed for quick action.
- Participation breeds commitment. Therefore, it is imperative to make sure that all parties (both suppliers and beneficiaries) take part in decision making. Most important is the need to involve the displaced, perhaps by emphasizing weekly meetings with popular leaders who understand the circumstances and attitudes of their people. These meetings should take place in every region with a large population of displaced people.

Chapter 8

# Operation Life-line Sudan and UNDP Programs for the Displaced

*Akram A. Eltom*

In this chapter I describe how the UN Development Program (UNDP), the UN Emergency Unit, and other UN bodies currently view the issue of displacement and its various ramifications. I touch only marginally on food aid, discussing instead the way displacement has challenged the entire UN system, forcing it to modify its mandate and development approach.

Since World War II, many international institutions have been established to bring economic assistance to developing countries. The majority are agencies in the UN system; and most, like UNDP, were designed to address the long-term needs of developing countries. Others, such as the Office of the UN High Commissioner for Refugees (UNHCR) and the UN Disaster Relief Office (UNDRO), were aimed at assisting countries affected by man-made or natural disasters. Within the past decade or so, the world has come to recognize the close relationship between disasters and development. Failing to address economic, social, and political needs increases the vulnerability of communities and countries to disaster, which in turn reduces their contributions to economic and social development. Despite the number of international, UN, bilateral, multilateral, and nongovernmental organizations charged with addressing these issues, persistent compartmentalization and the separation of disasters from their developmental context continue to hamper efforts.

Today, the UN system is changing to meet the changing needs of the world. One step has been its establishment of the Department of Humanitarian Assistance led by an undersecretary general in charge of emergency relief operations. Nevertheless, the UN system took four years to implement the idea, which was first suggested in the General Assembly in 1988, and even now the department does not really address the conflicting roles of some UN agencies. Still, strides have been made. Agencies such as UNDP are trying to abolish the idea of separating disaster and development and are exploring ways to combine their efforts. The task has been made easier by the fact that UNDP resident representatives in most parts of the world are charged with coordinating development in addition to serving as country coordinators for emergency and relief operations. In recognition of this step, the UN General Assembly declared in 1989 that as the relief process moves from immediate emergency response to the integration of displaced people into the economy, it will increasingly involve traditional development activities, which are the responsibility of UNDP and other entities of the UN system.

### UNDP's Mandate and Programs in the Sudan

Compared with the mandates of other UN agencies, the UNDP mandate is broad-based and relatively flexible. To fulfill part of its mandate, the agency aims multisectoral technical assistance at the most vulnerable groups in developing countries. This assistance almost invariably centers on projects carefully designed by UNDP. Grassroots community initiatives, women development activities, private-sector promotion, and environmental conservation all influence UNDP's choice of interventions, which must also be relevant to host government policies and needs. UNDP's approach generally emphasizes giving recipient governments and communities the tools to plan and execute their own developmental interventions.

In Sudan the sectoral distribution of UNDP's development assistance has shifted in the past decade toward strengthening economic planning capabilities, especially at the regional level, and increasing support for agricultural and rural development. During the most recent period of UNDP's assistance to Sudan (called the 1988–91 four-year country program cycle), the agency provided a total of $89.5 million to be used in projects. That sum included $45.5 million of government of Sudan/UNDP funds, called the indicative planning figure (IPF) and allocated by the UNDP governing council, and another $44 million from other sources but also administered by UNDP. The following list shows how those funds were allocated during Sudan's 1988–91 four-year country program cycle: area development schemes (ADS), 49 percent; rural resource use, 33 percent; regional planning, 14 percent; reserve, 3 percent; and other uses, 1 percent.

Of those categories, ADS is most immediately relevant to migration and rural development. Through ADS, pilot assistance has been directed to 420,000 people in selected rural communities in four regions of Sudan. Income-generating and production-oriented rural development interventions respond both to government emphasis and the actual needs of targeted communities. Improved living conditions, increased productivity, and increased family income are the projects' main themes. The ADS projects were designed to involve the target beneficiaries from design through implementation and evaluation; and despite some initial management problems, they have been a considerable success.

According to UNDP's country program, rural resource use is designed to help regional governments practice environmentally sound management of rural resources, particularly those related to water supply and desertification. Regional planning units strengthen regional planning capabilities. By supporting regional planning, UNDP intends to enable regional governments to identify development opportunities based on realistic strategies and reliable statistical data and to take advantage of those opportunities successfully.

Overall, UNDP's technical assistance totaled $19.5 million in 1987, or 2.4 percent of the total volume of external technical assistance. That total volume includes official development assistance from all donors but excludes all relief assistance and all assistance from NGOs.

## Recurrent Disasters in Sudan and UNDP's Immediate Response

In the process of working to implement interventions and programs, UNDP—and indeed the international community at large—came to realize that in a country like Sudan, which is continually racked by calamity, development assistance will fail if cycles of disaster are ignored. Since the 1970s, many factors, including political and economic constraints, have contributed to Sudan's inability to benefit from development assistance. Nevertheless, recurrent disasters such as war, tribal strife, drought, famine, floods, and displacement have continued to disrupt community socioeconomics and have hampered all government, agency, and donor attempts to address long-term developmental needs. Some of the many detrimental effects of this situation include the diversion of meager national resources to disaster relief; community upheaval resulting in the destruction of national production capabilities; disruption of the social, environmental, and economic fabric necessary for resource development; and a negative impact on development projects such as ADS.

All these issues warranted a major modification in UNDP's approach to Sudan, and the agency found no difficulty in carving a central role for itself. After studying the situation carefully, UNDP acknowledged that development should aim to prevent and alleviate the vulnerabilities constantly exposed by recurrent disaster.

## At a Crossroads

After Sudan's devastating 1984 famine, UNDP and the rest of the international community knew they needed to make a decision: should they continue to disregard the impact of recurrent disaster on development or contemplate a different approach to development and implement it as soon as possible? During the famine tens of thousands of Sudanese people died, more than two million were displaced from their homes, more than seven million people suffered from severe food shortages, and more than ten million farm animals were lost. Despite the tragedy, UNDP's relief effort was considered a notable success. The agency led the international community in coordinating the relief response, containing the devastation and mitigating what might have been a worse outcome.

In 1988 floods and torrential rains severely affected many parts of Sudan, including the capital city of Khartoum. UNDP assumed an aggressive role in combating the disaster, drawing on its mandate to coordinate international efforts to provide relief and emergency assistance. In an attempt to institutionalize the agency's role in disaster relief, the UNDP established its Emergency Unit (later the UN Emergency Unit) after an interagency mission in November 1988 identified urgent needs in Sudan. By successfully undertaking the flood assignment through its fledgling Emergency Unit, UNDP showed a pioneering approach to handling disaster in Sudan.

## Current Activities of UNDP and the UN Emergency Unit

Initially, the Emergency Unit's task combined relief, emergency rehabilitation, and development interventions aimed at improving the government's capacity to combat disasters. Refugees and the displaced were the unit's target populations. As mandated by a General Assembly resolution, UNDP and UNHCR helped Sudan cope with huge numbers of refugees from Ethiopia and other countries. The agencies and the government identified, formulated, and raised money for thirty-three projects in refugee-affected areas in Sudan. These projects required nearly $164 million in donor funding and were identified by Sudanese and international technical experts with the help of the Emergency Unit and UNHCR.

The 1988 interagency mission found weaknesses in Sudanese government institutions responsible for combating disaster situations. Therefore, the Emergency Unit is currently implementing projects to strengthen the Relief and Rehabilitation Commission (RRC), the Commission of the Displaced (COD), and the Ministry of Health. Furthermore, the unit is funding air relief efforts in war-affected southern Sudan and southwestern Kordofan and Darfur. In support of two pilot relocation schemes implemented by NGOs, the unit is administering funds from UNDP and cost-sharing sources. These schemes help war-displaced settlers integrate harmoniously into host communities. To prepare for future disasters in southwestern and western Sudan, UNDP has also funded a study to investigate the feasibility of a proposed base for relief operations in Babanousa.

## Operation Life-line Sudan

The UN Emergency Unit's best-known and most important activity is Operation Life-line Sudan (OLS), the first relief effort of its kind in history. In an operation mediated and coordinated by the UN, international humanitarian assistance has been channeled to civilian war victims through an agreement reached by both warring parties. After much heated negotiation, participants formulated a plan: eight river, road, train, and air routes were awarded temporary cease-fire status to allow relief to reach targeted populations in southern Sudan. These corridors of tranquility, as they were called, outlived phase 1 of OLS (which ended in December 1989) and became part of phase 2 (which ended in December 1990). During phase 2, OLS emphasized emergency rehabilitation needs in addition to relief assistance, with the goal of promoting self-reliance and preventing dependency.

OLS was able to deliver most of its committed assistance (totaling more than $100 million for both phases) within its planned time frame—in itself a success; and the operation has great potential as a model for future activities. Nevertheless, various publications, reviews, and statements have commented on shortcomings and negative aspects. For the most part, these comments reflect the opinions of participants, donors, UN agencies, the Sudan government, the Sudan People's Liberation Army (SPLA), and NGOs. For example, the warring factions are suspicious about an operation that requires any recognition, trust, or coordination with their foes. The donors are concerned about aid delivery and its material and political impact. While sharing some of the donors' concerns, the NGOs are also concerned about the constraints involved in implementing such a complicated operation.

The UN needed to coordinate, monitor, and supervise all aspects of OLS, taking into consideration individual sensitivities and constantly racing against time. It operated OLS through two coordination bases: one, a special coordinator linked to the UN Secretary General for Emergency and Relief Operations in Sudan; and the other, UNICEF's Nairobi office. Based in Khartoum, the special coordinator oversaw operations in government-held areas. UNICEF's Nairobi office, on the other hand, was responsible for coordinating relief operations in SPLA-held areas.

In addition to providing relief, OLS created an atmosphere that made proactive projects possible; and UNDP offered minimal but crucial developmental input to meet the recovery needs of war-affected populations during and after OLS. For example, in Wau, a government-held garrison town in southern Sudan, Emergency Unit field advisors identified the need to provide logistical and marketing support for small-scale groundnut farmers. UNDP responded by supplying bicycles so that farmers could market their produce and also helped to organize a farmers' cooperative. In another case, the Emergency Unit provided crucial support through aircraft operations, which were the only way to supply essential drugs to towns like Raga and Wau as well as seeds and tools to NGOs cultivating the thin safe zone around Juba. UNDP aircraft also offered logistical support to technical personnel from NGOs, the government, UNICEF, and the World Food Program, thus enabling these organizations to supervise projects. Similar strategies in Afghanistan and other countries have all been based on the OLS model and its lessons.

Despite these achievements, the fact remains that OLS and other relief efforts are temporary solutions to the problems facing Sudan's war-affected population. Before the people can be served in a comprehensive and sustainable way, there must be permanent peace in the country, which can be secured and maintained only when the political, economic, and social roots of underdevelopment and disaster are seriously addressed by the government and the international community.

### Recent UNDP Involvement in Specific Disaster-related Programs

In May 1990 the UNDP country program for 1988–91 was reviewed with the Ministry of Finance and Economic Planning in Khartoum. As a result, a fourth objective—emergency—was added to the other three (ADS, rural resource use, and regional planning). The emergency objective put ongoing UNDP disaster-relief efforts into a developmental context and laid the foundation for the Emergency Unit's mandate. To regularize UNDP's disaster-prevention and mitigation efforts, the emergency objective specified the unit's role:

a. As operational secretariat of the Special Coordinator for Emergencies the Unit will assist in the coordination of UN, donor, and NGO activities related to emergencies.

b. The Unit will assist the Government of Sudan in identifying and assessing the recurrent needs pertaining to any real or anticipated emergency situation and will help compile the information, analyze the data and present it to the international community to secure assistance.

c. While providing direct support in the above-mentioned point (b) the Unit will continue its institution-building interventions which are aimed at strengthening the government's capacity to coordinate, plan, and implement relief and emergency rehabilitation.

d. Closely related to point (c) above, the UN Emergency Unit will provide policy advice on issues related to migration and displacement, urban displaced, relocation and resettlement and will also assist the government of Sudan in formulating a national strategy for displaced persons issues.

e. To achieve the conceptual linkage between emergencies and development the UN Emergency Unit will continue to be involved in programming development assistance as one of the divisions of UNDP, and in this context will be instrumental in operational linkage of the emergency relief and rehabilitation interventions to the development process in the Sudan.

## The Special UN Drought Operations Support Program

The country program review enabled the UNDP to be more sensitive to Sudan's needs as they relate to a recurrent pattern of emergencies. In November 1990 UNDP collaborated with both the Ministry of Finance and Economic Planning and regional governments to conduct a series of evaluations aimed at focusing or modifying community-based projects to meet local needs created by drought and famine. After negotiating with regional and local authorities, evaluators modified several projects substantially and added more than $10 million to project budgets. All projects under review were scrutinized for design problems, implementation status, and constraints. In the end, food-for-work activities, village grain banks, and other food-related elements were added to the projects with the hope of impacting the population by the second quarter of 1991.

Collectively, these project-review activities became known as the Special UN Drought Operations Program (SUNDOS), a largely successful endeavor that UNDP is trying to extend. Through SUNDOS, UNDP was able to explore ways to bring disaster-threatened communities into the economic mainstream. The program has been scheduled for an in-depth review, giving UNDP an opportunity to improve problem definition and take a more meticulous approach to needs assessment. SUNDOS must also become better acquainted with the subtle and peculiar interaction between the political and socioeconomic influences exerted on target populations. A more holistic approach will draw on the sound principles of integrated rural community development to address health and educational needs. In addition, the program should develop an early-warning system focused on food insecurity, which may be linked with existing early-warning networks such as the countrywide RRC/FAO/USAID project and Darfur's ODA/Agricultural Planning Unit project.

UNDP is currently working on creative ways to implement area development schemes and has involved the World Bank, FAO, NGOs, and the Sudanese government. To fulfill its needs-assessment role, the Emergency Unit has responded to an RRC request and has conducted several joint RRC/UN/NGO needs-assessment missions to drought-affected areas and food-insecure regions in the south. After relief and rehabilitation needs are identified by the missions, help is solicited from the international community.

### Future Implications of UNDP's Role in Disaster Prevention

A disjointed approach to relief and development is inefficient and ultimately futile. Therefore, conceptual and strategic changes must forge a link between those two issues. Simply recognizing the link is not enough; real progress must involve changes in mandates, mission statements, and mentalities. For example, UNDP's assessment of need as well as political and socioeconomic potential should describe and analyze military and tribal conflict, which interacts with economic deprivation to create disaster situations and thus perpetuates poverty and suffering. It should also consider the geopolitical characteristics of a particular area that make it prone to disaster.

UN agencies should regard tribal and ethnic conflict as a preventable outcome and intervene to reduce the likelihood of conflict and alleviate its impact. Traditional strategies of avoiding conflict should be studied and then reinforced with current knowledge. In other words, improved skills, materials, and technology should be integrated with traditional norms and practices that are already working effectively.

A preventive approach to disaster has often been emphasized but rarely implemented. Because many disasters can be predicted, we must begin to prepare for them as early as possible. Furthermore, we must address gaps in equity and economic entitlement dictated by prevailing cultural and political values. By ensuring that UN projects have a sustainable impact, agencies can avoid thinking in terms of when and how the money flow can be terminated.

Before strategies can work, agencies need reliable information and statistics, which in a country like Sudan seem to be a luxury; in fact, they are a basic requirement for cementing the link between development and disaster. Therefore, we must design new sources of information and new methods for collecting data. In addition to reliable information, we need multidisciplinary and multisectoral collaboration among government institutions and related agencies. The existing situation dangerously hampers disaster response and delays any transition from emergency to normal conditions.

Many of these conceptual and strategic changes require institutional modifications before they can be implemented. Both nationally and globally, however, a major reorientation is taking place among UN policymakers, managers, and professionals. This reform also includes mandates, structure, legislation, administration, attitudes, management, monitoring skills, evaluation skills, and funding mechanisms—all are essential to success. These reforms are vital in today's changing world, especially in an institution that first developed during the 1940s and 50s.

## Conclusion

UNDP's problem-solving approach has changed as the world has changed. In particular, the agency now recognizes the strong link between disaster prevention and development. In response to the recurrent crisis in Sudan, the UNDP and the UN Emergency Unit have tried to address short-, medium-, and long-term dimensions of the problem rather than limit their interventions to disaster relief. There are enormous challenges, and the obstacles seem almost insurmountable. With determination, however, local communities, the Sudan government, and international agencies can do much to achieve this worthy goal.

Chapter 9

# Policy Lessons from the Displacement Problem in Sudan

*Eltigani E. Eltigani*

The chapters in this book have revealed the enormity of the displacement crisis in Sudan and have thoroughly analyzed the causes and implications of the policies designed to handle the problem. The enormity of the crisis is primarily an outcome of underdevelopment, misguided development policies, environmental degradation, and armed conflict.

Sudan's massive displacement problem and the way in which it has been handled have made many people skeptical about the government's fitness for handling the crisis. Red tape, lengthy procedures, unstructured and uninformed intervention exemplify the government's decision-making style. Because foreign and local NGOs have failed to overcome government ineptitude, they have not been able to do their jobs adequately.

I hope that Sudan's displacement crisis has given the country and others like it an insight into causes and implications. One important lesson is that policy approaches must be long term if the country is to combat the root of the problem. These long-term measures are necessary not only to fight the current crisis but also to prevent its recurrence. The following sections list a few of the many long-term approaches that may help to solve Sudan's displacement problem.

## Food Relief

Food relief may come from domestic sources if local efforts are mobilized or from external sources if the international community is mobilized. Food relief is essential to saving the lives of those at risk of starvation, particularly people living in the war zone. To be effective and cost-efficient, however, food relief should target only those in need to avoid creating a dangerous sense of dependency.

Food relief can be organized on a food-for-work basis, an approach that restores confidence, encourages responsibility and self-worth, and generates self-reliance among the displaced. The affected population should be involved in planning and implementing these work programs.

### Social Services

Disasters usually disrupt health, education, and other social services; therefore, providing social services in displaced settlements is extremely important. Medical care, sanitation, and clean water are essential to protecting both the settled and displaced populations against health problems caused by poor environmental and hygienic conditions.

Schools must be set up in displaced settlements and in settled communities affected by the influx of the displaced. By reducing the impact of displacement on education, the country can avoid giving settled children an advantage over displaced children.

### Relief Management

Because many people are skeptical about the efficiency and effectiveness of existing government relief institutions, it is necessary to create a disaster prevention and preparedness agency as an autonomous body in charge of relief and rehabilitation. This agency should work to decrease the vulnerability of disaster-prone areas and populations, become involved in promoting development in disaster-affected areas, and be able to respond swiftly to new emergency situations. It should also be equipped with efficient personnel, an advanced information system, and planning capabilities that allow it to meet the goals of its mandate.

Disaster prevention and preparedness committees formed at local and state levels should represent national and local governments, the community, and NGOs operating in affected areas. These committees should provide early warnings about disaster, contribute to food security, formulate disaster prevention and preparedness projects, and implement relief and rehabilitation projects that have been channeled through the committee structure.

### Ending the Civil War

The civil war is the prime cause of displacement among people in southern Sudan, and peace must be declared before the displacement problem can be resolved. Ending the war will alleviate the miseries suffered by civilian victims of the conflict and stop the drain of much-needed human, financial, and natural resources. Nevertheless, simply ending the war will not in itself solve the displacement crisis; reconstruction and development in war-affected areas are also vital.

### Development Strategies

Development strategies in Sudan should be designed to promote the following:

- Sudan must become self-reliant, particularly in food production; therefore, the government, local populations, and the international community should work hard to implement viable production strategies.
- A balanced development strategy can reduce and eliminate regional disparities in living standards and achieve a center-periphery equilibrium. Investment should aim to improve productivity in the traditional sector with the goal of increasing sustainable development.
- Sudan must use natural resources efficiently for development while preserving the environment—for example, by introducing environmental restoration programs into drought-devastated areas. Local communities should be involved in efforts to safeguard and restore the environment; and the design of development projects, particularly those involving large-scale mechanized farming, should consider how development will influence environmental degradation.

It is apparent that the displaced people are victims of bad policies and politics. It is therefore imperative to recognize that the population displacement problem cannot be seriously addressed without addressing the outstanding political and economic issues facing Sudan.

Finding an effective and practical solution to the many crises besetting the country, including the current displacement crisis, can only occur in an atmosphere of free debate and active participation in the design of the political and economic structures. This will lay the foundation for building a brighter future for Sudan.

# Notes

### Introduction

1. Francis M. Deng and Larry Minear, *The Challenges of Famine Relief Emergency Operations in the Sudan* (Washington, D.C.: Brookings Institute, 1992).

2. International Labour Organization, *Growth, Employment and Equity: A Comprehensive Strategy for the Sudan* (Geneva, 1976).

### Chapter 2: Displacement and Migration As a Consequence of Development Policies in Sudan

1. C. Meillassoux, "The Economy in Agricultural Self-sustaining Societies: A Preliminary Analysis," in *Relations of Production*, ed. David Seddon (Padstow, Eng.: T.J. Press, 1978).

2. Tony Barnett, *The Gezira Scheme: An Illusion of Development* (London: Cass, 1977).

3. T. Niblock, *Class and Power in Sudan: The Dynamics of Sudanese Politics, 1898–1985* (London: Macmillan, 1987).

4. L.S. is the abbreviation for the Sudanese pound. It equals one hundred piasters, or $3.33 in American dollars (according to the 1975 exchange rate).

5. Niblock, *Class and Power in Sudan.*

6. Ibid.

7. M.M. Abdel Salam, "Some Institutional Aspects and the Future of the Sudan Gezira Scheme" (DSRC Seminar Series, Discussion Paper 26, Khartoum, 1982).

8. Ibid.

9. I. A. Hassoun, "Western Migration and Settlement in Gezira," in vol. 33, *Sudan Notes and Records* (Khartoum, 1952).

10. M.E. Galal el Din and M.Y.A. El Mustafa, *Immigration and Internal Migration in Sudan* (in Arabic) (Khartoum: Khartoum University Press, 1979).

11. Hassaballa O. Hassaballa, "Social Change and Society Transformation in the White Nile Province: The Kenana Project" (Ph.D. diss., University of Washington, 1986).

12. Uma Lele, *The Design of Rural Development: Lessons from Africa* (Baltimore: Johns Hopkins University Press, 1975).

13. Hassaballa, "Social Change."

14. M.E. Galal el Din, *The Interaction Between Population and Development* (in Arabic) (Khartoum: Khartoum University Press, nd).

15. Commission of the National Capital, "Report of the National Capital Population Census" (Unpublished, Khartoum, 1989).

### Chapter 3: War Displacement: The Sociocultural Dimension

1. S.E. Ibrahim, "Peripheral Urbanism in the Sudan: Explorations into the Political Economy of the Wage Labour Market in Greater Khartoum, 1900–1984" (Ph.D. diss., University of Hull, 1985); "Theory and Ideology in Sudan Urban Studies: Towards a Critique of Peripheral Capitalist Urbanism," in *Perspectives on Development in the Sudan*. ed. Abdel Ghaffar M. Ahmed and Paul Van der Well (The Hague: Mouton Press, 1986).

2. National Dialogue Conference, "The Final Report of the Investigation Committee on the Impact of the Current War in the Country" (Khartoum, 1989).

3. MSF Holland, "The Conditions of the Displaced in Khartoum" (Unpublished report, Khartoum, 1988).

4. Ibid.

5. National Dialogue Conference, "The Final Report."

6. Ibid.

7. Mary Wani, "Women, Now the Sole Breadwinners," in *War Wounds: Development Costs of Conflict in Southern Sudan. Sudanese People Report on Their War*, ed. A. Abu Zeid et al. (London: Panos Institute, 1988).

8. K. Manibe, "The Agony of the Family," in *War Wounds*, ed. Zeid et al.

9. Ibid.

10. National Dialogue Conference, "The Final Report."

11. El Wathig Kameir and M. Babiker, "Coping Responses to the 1988 Floods Disaster: The Case of Deim Mayo" (Report presented to Oxfam America, 1990).

### Chapter 5: Health Implications of Displacement in Sudan

1. International Labor Organization, *Growth, Employment and Equity: A Comprehensive Strategy for the Sudan* (Geneva, 1976).

2. G. Solimano and G. Chapin, *The Impact of Socioeconomic Development and Ecological Change on Health and Nutrition in Latin America*, Cornell International Monograph Series, no. 9 (Ithaca: Cornell University Press, 1981).

3. B. Tekce and F. Shorter, "Determinants of Child Mortality: A Study of Squatter Settlements in Jordan," *Population and Development Review*, supp., 10 (1984): 257–80.

4. A. Farah and S. Preston, "Child Mortality Differentials in Sudan," *Population and Development Review* 8 (1982): 365–83.

5. Commission of the Displaced, "The Socioeconomic Consequences of Displacement" (Report presented at the National Conference on Displacement, Khartoum, 1990).

6. B. Winikoff, "Women's Health: An Alternative Perspective for Choosing Health Interventions" (Presented at the first annual conference of the Community Epidemiology/Health Management Network, Bangladesh, 15–19 November 1987).

7. K. Galway et al., *Child Survival: Risks and the Road to Health* (Columbia, Md.: Institute for Resource Development, 1987).

8. Ibid.

9. J.C. Waterlow et al., "The Presentation and Use of Height and Weight Data for Comparing the Nutritional Status of Groups of Children under the Age of 10 Years," *Bulletin of the World Health Organization* 55 (1977): 489–98.

10. Nutrition Department of the Ministry of Health, "Report on the Nutritional Monitoring Programme in the Displaced Settlements of Greater Khartoum, July 1990–July 1991" (Unpublished manuscript, Khartoum, 1991).

11. R. Myers and Cynthia Indriso, "Women's Work and Child Care," paper presented at a Rockefeller Foundation workshop, "Issues Related to Gender, Technology, and Development," Manila, the Philippines, 26–27 February 1987.

### Chapter 6: The Displaced, Food Production, and Food Aid

1. World Food Program, *Food Aid Review* (Rome: Food and Agriculture Organization, 1990).

2. A.G.M. Mohamed, "The Negative Impact of Emergency Food Aid on the Traditional Agricultural Production Systems in the Sudan," Environ-

mental Monograph Series, no. 7 (Khartoum: Institute of Environmental Studies, University of Khartoum, 1989).

3. Ibid.

## Chapter 7: Management of Relief for the Displaced

1. *Elingaz Elwatani* [newspaper], 17 May 1991.

# Selected Bibliography

Abu Sin, M. E. "Forms and Types of Disaster in Sudan." Paper presented to seminar on disaster prevention and management, University of Khartoum, 1990.

Barnett, Tony, and Abbas Abdelkarim, eds. *Sudan: State, Capital, and Transformation*. London: Croom Helm, 1988.

Bashir, M. Omer. *The Southern Sudan: Background to Conflict*. London: Hurst, 1968.

———. *The Southern Sudan: From Conflict to Peace*. London: Hurst, 1975.

De Waal, Alexander. *Famine That Kills: Darfur, Sudan, 1984–1985*. Oxford: Clarendon, 1989.

Garang, John. *The Call for Democracy in Sudan*. London: Kegan Paul International, 1991.

Khalid, Mansour. *Nimeiri and the Revolution of Dismay*. London: Kegan Paul International, 1985.

Simon, Maxwell, ed. *To Cure All Hunger: Food Policy and Food Security in Sudan*. London: IT Publications, 1991.

Teklu, Tesfaye, Joachim Von Braun, and El Sayed Zaki. "Drought and Famine Relationships in Sudan: Policy Implications." Research report no. 88, International Food Policy Research Institute, 1991.

Thomas, Graham. *Sudan 1950–1985: Death of a Dream*. London: Darf, 1990.

Voll, John, ed. *Sudan: State and Society in Crisis*. Bloomington: Indiana University Press, 1991.

Woodward, Peter. *Sudan after Nimeiri*. London: Routledge, 1991.

# Contributors

**M. E. Abu Sin** is an associate professor in the Department of Geography at the University of Khartoum.

**Omer Elmugly** is an assistant professor and dean of the Department of Economics and Rural Development at the University of Gezira.

**Eltigani E. Eltigani** is a population expert working for the Pan Arab Project for Child Development in Cairo. Previously, he was an assistant professor in the Population Studies Center at the University of Gezira.

**Akram A. Eltom** is a graduate student at Johns Hopkins University. He formerly worked with the UN Emergency Unit in Sudan.

**Carolyn Fluehr-Lobban** is a professor in the Department of Anthropology and Geography at Rhode Island College. She is a past president of the Sudan Studies Association.

**Hassaballa O. Hassaballa** is a research fellow on the Economic and Social Research Council in Khartoum.

**Salah El-Din El Shazali Ibrahim** is an associate professor working in the Development Studies and Research Center at the University of Khartoum.

**Hatim A. Mahran** is an assistant professor in the Department of Economics at the University of Gezira.

**Stephen A. Wol** works at the Ministry of Education and Instruction in Khartoum.

# Index

(Page numbers in italics refer to tables and figures.)